CATS' A–Z

Books by Beverley Nichols

PRELUDE
PATCHWORK
SELF
TWENTY-FIVE
CRAZY PAVEMENT
EVENSONG
ARE THEY THE SAME AT HOME?
THE STAR SPANGLED MANNER
WOMEN AND CHILDREN LAST
FOR ADULTS ONLY
FAILURES
CRY HAVOC!
THE FOOL HATH SAID
NO PLACE LIKE HOME
NEWS OF ENGLAND
MESMER
GREEN GROWS THE CITY
REVUE
THE GIFT OF A GARDEN
THE GIFT OF A HOME
NO MAN'S STREET
THE MOONFLOWER
MEN DO NOT WEEP
VERDICT ON INDIA
THE TREE THAT SAT DOWN
ALL I COULD NEVER BE
THE STREAM THAT STOOD STILL
SHADOW OF THE VINE
THE MOUNTAIN OF MAGIC
PILGRIM'S PROGRESS
THE SWEET AND TWENTIES
CATS' A.B.C.
CATS' X.Y.Z.
GARDEN OPEN TODAY
POWERS THAT BE
A CASE OF HUMAN BONDAGE
GARDEN OPEN TOMORROW
THE ART OF FLOWER ARRANGEMENT
THE SUN IN MY EYES
FATHER FIGURE
DEATH TO SLOW MUSIC
THE RICH DIE HARD
MURDER BY REQUEST
DOWN THE KITCHEN SINK

BEVERLEY NICHOLS'

Cats' A–Z

Illustrated by Derrick Sayer

W. H. ALLEN · LONDON
A Howard & Wyndham Company
1977

Beverley Nichols' Cats' A–Z is made up of two previously published books:
Beverley Nichols' Cats' A.B.C.

Beverley Nichols' Cats' X.Y.Z.

Printed and bound in Great Britain by
Butler & Tanner Ltd, Frome and London,
for the Publishers, W. H. Allen & Co. Ltd,
44 Hill Street, London W1X 8LB

ISBN 0 491 02351 0

My thanks are due to the following for permission to quote the verses included in this book: the Author's Representative and Sidgwick & Jackson Ltd for the extract from 'Dining-Room Tea' from *Collected Poems of Rupert Brooke*; the Trustees of the Hardy Estate and Macmillan & Co., Ltd for two verses from 'Lines to a Dumb Friend' by Thomas Hardy from *Collected Poems*; The Cresset Press for the lines from 'To a Caged Lion' by Ruth Pitter from her book *On Cats*; and Chapman and Grimes Inc., Boston, U.S.A., for the verse by Muriel Schulz quoted on page 107—this is from their publication *Sophisti-Cats*, compiled and edited by Lynn Hamilton; the Trustees of the Hardy Estate and Macmillan & Co. Ltd for the lines from 'Last Words to a Dumb Friend' from *The Collected Poems of Thomas Hardy*; The Bodley Head Ltd for the lines from *The Sphinx* by Oscar Wilde; and Chapman and Grimes Inc., Boston, U.S.A., for the verses 'Wind is a cat' by Ethel Romig Fuller and 'I have no pets to hold my heart' by Helen Maring, both from their publication *Sophisti-Cats*, compiled and edited by Lynn Hamilton.

For Jeannie
and Derek Tangye
with purrs

Foreword

In the original editions of this book I suggested that the human race could be divided into two sections—F and non-F, Feline or non-Feline. This meant that every child, at birth, is endowed with characteristics which entitle it to claim membership of the Honourable Company of Cats or the equally Honourable Company of Dogs. I also suggested that this theory has a sound psychological basis, that it was not just a fashionable quirk, like U and non-U, but that it had its roots deep in the mysteries of human nature and had a universal application, particularly when one applies it to the arts. Thus, Chopin was F and Beethoven was non-F. Fragonard and Corot were F, Rembrandt and Rubens were non-F. I have never been sure about Picasso, though he has his F moments. The theory can even be applied to politics. One of the most F geniuses who ever purred his way to power was Disraeli. One of the least F was Gladstone.

Is this merely a parlour game? Yes, and no. For although it may be an amusing subject of discussion on dull winter evenings it can hardly be denied that in our attitude to animals, our response to them and their response to ourselves, we reveal significant traits of our own personalities. In so wide a subject, which borders on the realm of mysticism, it is impossible to lay down strict definitions but as a general rule I would suggest that F people are more sensitive, more perceptive and certainly more independently minded than non-F people; and that for this reason they have a great deal to teach us, if we study them intelligently. This can certainly not be claimed for dogs, who have nothing to teach us at all. Why? Because dogs are basically a slower race, which is almost certainly why they are so cherished by the great majority of their owners. Any man however depraved, any woman however worthless, can command the adoration of a dog, at the flick of a finger. They have only to shout 'to heel' and the poor creature stops in its tracks, and grovels until it is allowed to get up again. Such conduct on the part of a cat is quite unthinkable. It would merely stare at you in pained astonishment and walk away.

How are we to account for this extraordinary difference? My own theory is that it lies in the fact that every cat is essentially an aristocrat. However humble its surroundings, however harsh the blows that life has dealt in the alleys and the back streets, it is aware, however dimly, that there is royal blood in its veins. There is really no such thing as an 'alley-cat' in the accepted sense of the word. Always, even when it is faint with hunger, it will move with grace, and even when it is faced with the hostility of the human race, it will look the enemy straight in the eyes.

A cat appears on page one of a book called *Prelude*, the first novel I ever published, at the age of nineteen, more than half a century ago. When one is nineteen one naturally assumes that one knows as much about life as is worth knowing—which may indeed be true—and that one had better get it down on paper before it is too late.

Well, I have been celebrating my love of cats ever since, and the essence of that love is to be found in the following pages. I hope that it may have something to teach you about these enchanting creatures that you did not know before. And quite possibly, whether you are F or non-F, it might even have something to teach you about yourself.

In pages so light-hearted as these it might seem incongruous to introduce a serious note. But if you love cats at all, and delight in their companionship, they come to mean more to you than mere 'pets', they are *persons* in their own right. They should be treated as such. And there are two aspects in the average cat owner's attitude which have always disturbed me. Both of them are, quite literally, matters of life and death.

The first concerns the sad necessity which is usually described as 'putting them to sleep'. This is a polite euphemism for killing them. I do not think that my views on this subject are fanatical; I have always been a staunch believer in the doctrines of voluntary euthanasia for all human beings, including myself. I did not ask to come into this world and it is the height of impertinence that anybody should dictate to mè the manner or the moment when I leave it, should life become intolerable.

But only too often cat-owners—I will not call them cat-lovers—approach the problem with appalling flippancy. They are moving from a house to a flat; or they are going away for a long holiday. What is to be done about poor pussy? Very sad, of course, but not to worry. She can always be 'put to sleep'. So one day the vet calls, and she is lifted into his arms, and there is the prick of a needle, and a little life is ended—a life that might have been long and happy.

This seems to be quite inexcusable. If people are not prepared to look after animals properly, in sickness or in health, for better or for worse, they should not have animals at all. In the long catalogue of my cat-life there have been only two occasions when I have been compelled to put them to sleep, and in both cases the decision was inevitable. The first concerned a tabby called Four, who figures in these pages. When the vet came, I held him in my arms in the last moments. I felt like a murderer but . . . well . . . Four was twenty-one years old, which for a human-being would make him a centenarian, and he was already on the way out. The other cat was Oscar, who also plays a part in this book. Oscar was only eleven but he was desperately ill with cancer, and his mind was going. I had not the guts to hold him in my arms; it would have been unendurable. Instead—at the risk of sounding ridiculous—I went to church and said a prayer. I like to think that if our roles had been reversed, he would have done the same for me.

The other 'matter of life and death' which all cat-lovers should at least consider, whatever they may decide to do about it, concerns the delicate matter of neutering, which is usually disguised by the polite euphemism . . . 'having them arranged'. This is another problem which most cat-owners treat with flippancy. I cannot do so. After all, when you neuter a cat you are, in a way, cutting its life in half, you are denying its birthright. I am not perhaps the most suitable person to discuss this question because in the present state of the world, when countless millions of babies are born to parents who have nothing to offer them but a brief life of misery and starvation, I strongly suspect that it might be an excellent idea if the majority of mankind were castrated at birth. Also, I have more than a little sympathy with Voltaire, who once observed that men would not have love-affairs at all if they had not first read about them. Or words to that effect.

This is one of those problems on which we must make up our own minds. My own feeling is that if you have a cat neutered you must make recompense, you must give it something in return—security, understanding and, of course, love. You have deprived it of one sort of love, you must be very sure that it is not starved of the other.

I said above that if you study cats you will discover a great deal not only about them but about yourself. What you may learn may not always be to your liking, if you have the patience and the honesty to accept the message which shines so clearly from their eyes. I can only say that without them my life would have been very much the poorer. There would have been less laughter, fewer excitements; there would have been an emptiness in the garden and a loneliness in the house. Above all, there would have been less of the mystery which they always engender, wherever they may go.

We live in an age when we flatter ourselves that we have solved most of the enigmas of the universe, even the ultimate enigma of the human soul. But there is one mystery that we still never solve—the mystery of the cat. I have tried to do so, and sometimes I believe that I have had some success. But there is still much to learn. Till the end of time, only cats will hold the answer to the riddle of the Sphinx.

Beverley Nichols
1977

A stands for Amusements.

We must be brutally frank, from the very outset, about the whole business of playing with cats and kittens. Many persons who think themselves impeccably F have in fact little understanding of it.

Let us take as a simple example the familiar device of a length of string to which we attach a screwed-up piece of paper, in order to simulate a mouse. A regrettably large proportion of cat-owners, having manufactured this elementary form of diversion, seem to imagine that nothing remains to be done but to drag the string languidly across the carpet, giving it an occasional twitch, while the cat or kitten leaps and pounces and cavorts in its wake.

This is surely the most stingy and unimaginative behaviour; it is totally lacking in drama, and drama is the essence of all feline diversion. Even as he ties the paper to the string the cat-owner should become tense, his fingers should tremble slightly, and he should cast occasional sidelong glances towards the cat, who will be regarding him with cool concentration, appraising his performance. (All cats are dramatic critics, just as all dramatic critics are cats.)

The device completed, a few final moments of psychological 'conditioning' are advisable. Holding the string in his hands the true F should say to himself: 'I am no longer the owner of a pleasing furry quadruped, who is about to romp round the room, I am now in actual fact a mouse.' Whereupon he must shrink, and shrink, and go on shrinking, with increasing alarm, transmitting his emotions down the string as though it were a telegraph wire, until the paper at the other end is impregnated with his personality. He may then, in a mouse-like manner, twitch the string, at the same time closing his eyes, gritting his teeth and awaiting the Pounce of Doom.

(Practical Note. While these manœuvres are *en train* it is as well to lock the door. To be suddenly wrenched back into the world of humans, when one has successfully shrunk, is most disturbing to the nervous system.)

All is now in readiness for the actual performance. This is best given in a large house, where there is a wide staircase, so that the string may be trailed up and down, step by step, and occasionally swung through the banisters. All cats have a curious passion for banisters, and some of the pleasantest moments in my life have been spent pushing little pieces of paper, feathers, pencils and such-like through the banisters of an old Georgian house, for the delectation of 'One',[1] my first Siamese—now, alas, departed from this world.

[1] For an explanation of the numerical names of my cats, please turn to page 73. B.N.

Talking of 'One' reminds me of a favourite diversion of all Siamese cats, which seems to be little known even in the best F circles . . . Backsliding. I discovered this by accident. One winter evening 'One' was lying on his back enjoying the warmth of a blazing log fire. His front legs were stretched out at full length behind him, his head lolled to one side, and though at first he seemed to be asleep he was in fact regarding me out of the corner of one blue eye. It was, in short, an attitude of allurement, but I could not interpret it. What was required? Tummy-rubbing? Chin-stroking? Neither of these seemed to meet the case. Then I put my hand on his chest and gave him a slight push backwards. Immediately his eyes opened and he registered an expression of delight. I pushed again, a little farther. The delight increased to ecstasy, and he remained on his back, with his paws dangling in front of him. So I increased the pressure, crawling on my knees beside him, pushing him backwards against the pile of the carpet. Every time that I paused for lack of breath he stayed stock still, demanding more.

Presumably the sensation of the carpet rubbing against his spine was like a sort of super-stroke. Whatever the reason, it became a 'must' in 'One's' programme of amusement. As time went on we became increasingly expert, and since we both had implicit trust in one another, the Backsliding developed many brilliant variations—under the piano, and through the legs of chairs. It was even practised in the kitchen, which was covered with linoleum, so that 'One' could be catapulted across it for distances of up to ten feet.

I should hesitate to publish this diversion to the world without the accompanying diagram, which shows the correct position in which the hand should be placed. If it is too high, pussy will choke; if it is too low, no proper balance can be achieved, and pussy will give the same sort of dirty look as I once observed on the face of a famous ballerina, when her partner was fiddling about with the wrong part of her waist during a difficult passage of *Swan Lake*. And even with the diagram, another word of warning must be spoken. Elderly Siamese cats, who have graced households where Backsliding is not practised, may—on a first introduction—be puzzled and even faintly outraged if one attempts to explain it to them. So, indeed, may their owners. More than one foolish woman, on seeing me initiate her pet in this charming pastime, has protested that I am hurting pussy, or frightening her, or some such grotesque suggestion. But if I am only given one minute—no more—in which to explain the elements, even the most respectable dowager Siamese will succumb, and will recline in the centre of the Aubusson, paws dangling, asking . . . no, positively demanding . . . that the Backsliding should continue.

Backsliding, as we have observed, is almost exclusively a Siamese taste; the average tabby will have none of it. Even the gentlest attempt to teach the elements of Backsliding to the ordinary cat is doomed to failure. Pussy will curl into a protesting ball of fur, and if the worst comes to the worst, pussy will scratch.

Most feline amusements, such as ping-pong balls, are enjoyed by every variety of cat. For example, I have yet to meet the cat which does not throw itself whole-heartedly into the Newspaper Game. This requires two or more players—perhaps the ideal number is three—and no apparatus except a few sheets of newspaper. Any newspaper will do, though my own cats, who are inclined to be

choosy, seem to prefer the *Financial Times*. The procedure is simple. The largest and most docile of the players is placed in the centre of the carpet, and gently covered with a sheet of newspaper. If the newspaper does not entirely cover the cat, a second sheet may be added, so that pussy is completely invisible with the exception of the tip of her tail. It is important that this should remain uncovered.

'But this is absurd!' the non-F may exclaim. 'Covering an animal with a newspaper and expecting it to stay still! Who ever heard of such a thing? If I were to try such tricks with my dog ...' To which I would retort: 'We are not suggesting that this game should be played with dogs. Nor with elephants nor with eagles. But it can, and should, be played with cats ... with all cats, that is to say, who have been treated as equals, if not as superiors.'

This may be a strange fact, but it is a fact. Covered by her canopy of the *Financial Times*, pussy remains as still as a graven image. The other players may now be placed in strategic positions. For a few moments there will be silence and an atmosphere of unbearable tension. Then the pussy under the newspaper gives a sharp twitch with her tail, indicating that she is ready. Whereupon, almost immediately, one of the players will pounce, and the game has begun. Experienced pouncers will probably land on the edge of the newspaper, and then beat a rapid retreat. Sometimes they may not pounce at all, preferring to stalk and dab, in the manner of matadors. Kittens usually pounce rather too soon, and sometimes, not quite getting the hang of it, they push their noses under the paper and are pounced on in their turn. But if the game is skilfully played, with suitable co-operation from the cat-owner in the matter of readjusting the newspaper when it slips off pussy's back, it will provide moments of the greatest excitement, and by the end of it the room will be littered with scraps of newspaper and Gaskin will have to come in with the Hoover.

Strange as it may seem—or is it so strange?—many cats greatly enjoy taking part in games which are usually regarded as for humans only, such as playing patience. I play a great deal of patience during my work, usually about six games to the morning; when one's invention is flagging a game of patience is like a pause by the wayside to regain one's wind. In these games I am greatly assisted—though perhaps that is not quite the word—by 'Five', particularly if he has just come in from the garden with muddy paws. Indeed, 'Five' has left so many paw-prints on my various packs of cards that I am able to cheat with comparative ease.

Then there is that very soothing game called Scrabble. My cat Oscar is a keen Scrabble player. This game, in my house, is conducted on a large circular Regency table with a glass top, and as soon as Oscar hears the clatter of the counters he leaps on to the table, eager to join the party. Normally he keeps his enthusiasm within bounds, contenting himself with an occasional dab at the pool of counters, which sends a few of them on to the floor. There have been occasions, however, when he is less restrained, and attacks the board itself. I shall never forget the time when a somewhat frenzied female guest, at the end of the game, had triumphantly placed the letter Z on a treble square, and having done so, proceeded to add the letters ITH. But that was as far as she got. For Oscar, misinterpreting her gestures, chose that moment to give the board a sharp swipe, which scattered the whole pattern in hopeless confusion. 'That monstrous cat of yours!' cried the lady. 'It was going to have been ZITHER and it would have been a treble and it would have won me the game.' I pointed out that it would, in fact, have done nothing of the sort, for the letters ZI would have clashed with the letters QU in the next row, and there was, as far as I was aware, no word even remotely resembling ZIQU in current use in the English language. (After a long course of Scrabble, and a great deal of reference to the *Oxford Dictionary*, I am not so sure about that last remark. I should not be surprised to look up ZIQU and find that it was, in fact, a rare but amiable form of antelope, native of Formosa.)

Perhaps you do not play Scrabble. In which case I fear that this story will have bored you. So let us leave the house and wander into the garden.

I often think that the ideal setting for outdoor feline sport is the orchard. (Except during the months of September and October, when the grass is scattered with windfalls. For with the windfalls come the wasps, and there have been occasions when pussy has sniffed a wasp, with disastrous and melodramatic results.) But if it is the month of May, when the blossom is out, and if one is accompanied by a white Persian kitten, which allows itself to be lifted on to a lower branch, in order to dab at twigs, moments of the utmost enchantment are almost certain to ensue. There is only one disadvantage to this pastime. The kitten is so exquisite, the apple-blossom is so liltingly beautiful, the white clouds scudding across the sky are so charged with the winds of poetry, the whole design, in short, is so stunningly photogenic—including, one trusts, one's own profile in the bottom left-hand corner—that one feels self-conscious, as though one were posing for the cover of a Christmas calendar. Which, now I come to think of it, might not be such a bad idea.

B stands for Beeing.

The spelling will explain itself in a moment. For B also stands for beetling and butterflying. And for a great many other things which do not begin with B, such as hedgehogging, and dragonflying and spidering and goldfishing and—though it sounds almost unbearably whimsical—for daddy long-legging, or as the Germans might say, *Grossvaterbeinenspiel.* And—here we have a sigh—B also stands for mousing.

The problem of the cat and the mouse is one that has been argued between Fs and non-Fs since time immemorial. The non-Fs cite it as one of the reasons why they dislike cats. Whereupon, the Fs feel very uncomfortable and try to gloss over the subject with vague references to 'Nature'.

Personally I should have thought that this was one of those problems which might reasonably be deposited, fairly and squarely, on the lap of the Almighty, who—with all deference—can hardly evade all responsibility. However, before doing so, let us consider a few facts. Let us clear our minds by studying the behaviour of my own cats, 'Four', 'Five' and Oscar.

Never was there a less bloodthirsty trio. Perhaps it would be unbecoming of me to suggest that this may be because they have inherited some of the amiable characteristics of their master. (The only blood-sport in which I ever indulge is Flitting Flies and even then I have some qualms of conscience, particularly in the case of very large black flies that refuse to swoon swiftly away, but lie buzzing on their backs and then suddenly get up again and swoop dizzily across to the other end of the room. For this reason I usually supplement the Flit gun with a whisk, in order to ensure a speedy dispatch.)

But though my cats are exceptionally unpredatory, they *are* cats, with the instinct of hunting, which must have an occasional outlet. But instead of chasing mice, rats or any of the conventional quarries, they usually choose very different objects. Hence the expression—Beeing.

Beeing was invented by 'Five', in the days when I had a large bed of heather outside the window of my music room. 'Five' used to play in this heather when he was a kitten; it was a lovely place for bounding about on, like an immense feather bed; and some of it was tall enough for him to imagine that he was in a jungle. Then one day in early spring the sun came out hot and strong, and since there was still plenty of *erica carnea* in flower, the bees arrived in hosts. They went to 'Five's' head in more senses than one, but fortunately we had somebody staying who understood the technique of sting-removing and of bathing 'the affected part' with bicarbonate of soda. As time went on, 'Five' became more cunning. He treated the bees rather as though they were tennis balls being sent over the net by a pro, sitting quite still and giving them an occasional sharp bash

with a closed paw, which sent them reeling indignantly into a mound of pink blossom. Stings were few and far between. All the same whenever 'Five' stalked out to his vantage point in the heather I would send a warning message to Gaskin: '"Five" is Beeing, be ready with the bicarbonate.'

Now consider 'Four'. He has no feeling about bees at all. Even if you were to sit him in front of a large snapdragon when immense bumble-bees were pushing their gold-dusted bottoms through the velvet curtains—like very fat ladies negotiating revolving doors—'Four' would be quite unmoved. For 'Four' is almost exclusively a fisherman.

In every garden I have ever owned there has been a lily pond, for a garden without water is like a room without a looking glass; the sheet of water, even if it is only a tiny one, seems to smile up to the sky, and the sky smiles back, and there you are, with a little patch of heaven on the lawn. But by the side of this patch of heaven, unfortunately, there is usually to be found a small black imp, fishing. 'Four' practises this art with skill and intelligence. He has learned how to place himself so that his shadow does not fall athwart the water. He has also learned that there are certain clumps of water grasses which conceal him from detection by anybody looking through the windows of the house. He sits stock-still—not even the twitch of a tail. In spite of this, he seldom catches anything, and I could count on the fingers of one hand the occasions when a small, golden, and rather gruesome corpse has been deposited outside the back door as a proof of his prowess.

As for Oscar—he is is primarily a bird-watcher, with the accent very much on the word 'watching'. He sits at the window making the most gruesome castanet noises with his teeth. If looks could kill there would not be a sparrow left in Surrey. Every time I see this savage demeanour I am reminded of a certain performance of *Norma* at La Scala in Milan, with Callas in the leading role. I watched this charming old *marron glacé* of an opera from a box in which I was flanked by two rival prima donnas. At the ovation which greeted the end of the aria 'Casta Diva' the faces of these two ladies wore expressions exactly like Oscar's when he is bird-watching; they were contorted with rage and envy and the most fiendish malice; and if Madame Callas had been a bird, her days would have been short indeed.

But the mouse is waiting, as it were, in the wings, the symbol of the eternal argument between Fs and non-Fs. I suggested above that this was a problem which might be deposited in the lap of the Almighty, like all other problems involving the basic sin of cruelty. If this sounds to the non-Fs as though I were evading the issue, let me suggest that we send it instead to the members of the Loamshire Stag-Hunting Association, or some similar collection of primitive barbarians. Stag-hunting is a purely human pastime. It is carried on, with the hysterical co-operation of hounds—'dogs are so much more sporting than cats!'—solely for the purpose of amusement. It has not the primary excuse, which can be made for all animals, that its members are obeying an ancient instinct that compels them to kill in order to eat. It is cruelty, naked and unadorned, and before the non-F begins to attack pussy for chasing her mouse, I would suggest that he begin to put his own human house in order.

All the same, on the very rare occasions when my own cats discover a mouse, there is an immediate crisis, a frenzied rushing hither and thither and an appalling expenditure of nervous energy.

How do *you* deal with a mouse crisis? What do you do if you suddenly look out of the window and see, to your dismay, that It has happened again . . . that pussy is doing this terrible *danse macabre* on the lawn, pouncing and retreating and cavorting? (Though I appear to be censuring pussy I cannot refrain from reminding non-Fs that her demeanour, even in such moments, contrasts very favourably with that of Salome.)

My own actions depend entirely on whether Gaskin is in or out. If he is in I rush to the kitchen and break the news. 'Four' has a mouse. It is on the lawn. It is in the shrubbery. Or worst of all, it is actually being transported towards the back door. Does Gaskin think that he could possibly . . . ? Gaskin sighs, wipes his hands, folds up a dish-cloth, takes a small frying-pan from the rack, and departs, to deal with the situation. Five minutes later he returns, having dealt with it. The mouse has escaped. No, it was *not* hurt and 'Four' has been shut up in the toolshed to calm down. Or the mouse was already dead, and partially devoured, and 'Four' will almost certainly be sick. (Serve him right, one thinks.) Or the mouse was alive, but swiftly dispatched with the frying-pan.

After which, the household gradually reverts to normal.

If Gaskin is out, things are not so easy. I should be little use with the frying-pan, though in the last extremity I might resort to it. And so my principal weapon is vocal. Yells and roars and shouts and imprecations, as I chase pussy across the lawn or through the shrubbery. In any ordinary household these tactics might not work. But my cats are so used to deference, they are so accustomed to gentle accents, that when they suddenly see me rushing after them, bellowing like a bull, they experience a shock of such acute astonishment that the mouse is usually abandoned. Which means, of course, that one crisis is immediately supplanted by another. For though the mouse is saved, pussy has fled in alarm, and one is immediately haunted by the thought that she has gone for good, and has set out on some lonely, fateful journey through the lanes and the hedgerows where she will eventually starve to death. These are times when I think it would be really much less exhausting to keep tortoises.

Only once did the vocal tactics cause embarrassment. The mouser was Oscar and Gaskin was not at hand. I shot out, as usual, roaring and cursing, while Oscar carried out evasive tactics in the hedge. 'Put it down!' I yelled. Bellow, bellow, bellow. 'Stop it at once!' Bang, bang, bang with a brick on the frying-pan. 'Put that wretched thing *down*!' Unfortunately the hedge skirted a lane down which, at that very moment, the ladies of the local Conservative Association were marching, grim-faced, on their way to a meeting at the village hall. They were carrying a blue banner embroidered with the words For Queen and Country. They misinterpreted my action and I was never asked to open their garden fête again.

C stands for Cuisine.

Every pussy, if given a chance, is an epicure. The pussy who has been brought up with love and understanding never gobbles her food, and though on rising from the table she may not send her compliments to the chef in so many words, she makes it very clear if she has been pleased or not. Even non-Fs will agree that this demeanour is in striking contrast to the behaviour of dogs, who gulp their meals in a grossly animal manner, and very seldom complain even if they are offered the sort of fare which used to be provided on British Railways. In which their conduct strikingly resembles that of their masters.

My own cats have always been fortunate in the fact that they have been served by a first-class chef in the form of Gaskin. He takes as much trouble with their meals as with mine, and would be as distressed if their whiting were not *à point* as if my *soufflé* had failed to rise. I need hardly say that in the course of twenty-five years neither of these disasters has yet occurred.

Moreover, Gaskin takes almost as much trouble with what might be called the general arrangements of the table as with the actual preparation of the dishes. Thus, he regards placing as of vital importance. Many of us have probably attended dinner parties in Paris where there have been frightful *froideurs* about procedure, when some obscure but legitimate count has threatened to leave the room because he has been placed in an inferior position to an equally obscure, but bastard, marquis. Throughout history, members of the French aristocracy have always been so busy fussing about where they sit at table that they usually have failed to notice that the entire country is sinking rapidly into the abyss. Gaskin's seating arrangements for the pussies arise from no such foolish snobbishness; he has merely learned, from long experience, that there are certain places where they like to dine and certain places where they do not, and that is that. Why they have chosen these places, nobody knows, and as far as I am aware, nobody has ever been so vulgar as to ask them.

Thus, 'Four' insists on breakfasting under the kitchen sink, 'Five' on the kitchen table, and Oscar in a corner by the side of the dresser. Were the plates to be placed in any other position, they would be ignored. There would be pained expressions, lashings of the tail, shruggings of the shoulders, and exits into the garden, and no food would be partaken until Gaskin had come to his senses.

This fastidiousness has its drawbacks. There have been a few unhappy occasions when I have been abroad, and when Gaskin has gone away for the night. Needless to say, before doing so he has engaged a reliable woman as a 'temporary' to attend to the cats' menus. He has inquired into her antecedents, vetted her character, and thoroughly coached her in the technique. The fish must be cooked just so long, and no more. The milk must be warmed. There must be a large bowl of fresh water. The times for breakfast and dinner must be strictly observed: 7·45 for breakfast, 4·15 for dinner. Above all, the position of the plates must never vary ... 'Four' under the sink, 'Five' on the kitchen table, and Oscar by the dresser. 'You understand?' says Gaskin. Yes, says the temporary, she understands. Whereupon Gaskin, with a last beetling glance, hands her the latch-keys and departs, not without forebodings.

Alas, the forebodings have sometimes been justified. Even reliable women, with clean aprons and rosy faces, may have a sinister streak of non-Fness in their characters. Such a one was Mrs ... never mind, we will call her Mrs X. How was Gaskin to know that Mrs X, who had impeccable references, with duchesses raving about her *soufflés* across pages of coroneted writing paper, could possibly be so wickedly incompetent about feeding the cats? No—it was not incompetence, it was done with deliberation. For Mrs X, arriving on the following morning in the empty house—admittedly on time—suddenly decided that the cats were 'pampered'. (In subsequent cross-examination she actually *confessed* to this.) And so, having cooked the fish, she set it all on a large plate in the centre of the floor and left the cats to it, under the astonishing impression that they would eat it. She had some odd, barbaric notion that she was 'teaching them a lesson'. I am not suggesting that she was actually a sadist, and I believe that she was quite a good mother to her own three very plain and sniffly children who would probably have eaten with the greatest relish off a communal plate in the middle of the floor. All the same, I really do think it a great pity that there should be such women in the world.

Cats, of course, have exquisite table manners, though their etiquette differs somewhat from the more restricted human variety. I wonder if any of the following customs are shared by the pets of other Fs?

1. Dabbing. This is permissible in the best circles. My own principal dabber is 'Five'. He usually decides to dab when offered a small

piece of the dish one is eating oneself. He enters the dining-room, sits by one's chair, and subjects one to a steady stare. Needless to say, he would never do anything so impolite as to mew, or to reach up to the table. The stare is duly rewarded by a small portion of chicken or steak or whatever one may be eating. This is cut up, as a *bonne bouche*, and placed before him. Whereupon 'Five' lowers his head and contemplates the *bonne bouche*. This contemplation may last for several minutes. 'Really, "Five", you are a spoilt cat,' one says. 'That is a beautiful piece of chicken. There are many cats, sleeping on the Embankment, who would be most grateful for ...' But one does not finish the sentence, for if one begins to think of cats sleeping on the Embankment one will have a wretched night and get no sleep oneself. However, the reproof seems to have registered, for 'Five' suddenly emerges from contemplation and gives the piece of chicken a sharp dab with his right paw. It slides to the edge of the plate; then it is dabbed back again with the left paw. For all I know, this may be 'Five's' retort to one's remark about the Embankment; it may be his way of saying that such painful subjects should not be mentioned at meal times. Whatever the reason, he eventually eats the piece of chicken. Having done so, he sits down and makes his toilet. He never asks for more.

2. Growling. This habit may seem to non-Fs to conflict with the claim for 'exquisite table manners'. I do not think so, for two reasons. Firstly, because there is only one dish—at least as far as my own cats are concerned—which gives rise to growling ... rabbit. Why this should be, I do not pretend to understand. I can only register the fact that when rabbit is on the menu, growls are in the air. They are very fierce growls, accompanied by dramatic movements of the head over the shoulder, as though seeking some imaginary enemy.

The other reason why I am, as it were, pro-growling, is because I think it would greatly enliven human dinner parties if it were generally adopted. I would not growl over most of the dishes one is offered in British households, but I would certainly growl over caviare. If one is the least important guest, as one usually is, and if one is sitting in Starvation Corner, and if one sees great dollops of this ambrosia being ladled out to fat rich ladies who could well afford to buy it by the bucket, and if one is eventually given a tiny reluctant scraping from the bottom of the jar . . . surely one *should* growl? One should not only growl, but scratch and pounce and hiss. One dies, in spirit, but not in fact, and repression, as we all know, ties the psyche up in knots.

3. Leaving a small piece uneaten. All delicately nurtured felines do this. It is the ultimate proof of good breeding. Even if one adopts the scruffiest alley cat, as soon as he has been plumped out and given the blessed assurance that his days of scrummaging in dustbins are over, he will leave a little bit of dinner uneaten. I have never known any exceptions to this rule. It is absolutely *de rigueur*, and it suggests that somewhere, in the Feline Archives, there must be some venerated volume of Etiquette for Cats, thumbed by countless paws and sniffed over by hosts of little noses, whose lessons are passed down from generation to generation.

D stands for Dilapidations.

If Oscar were a human I should send him a small bill for the current year. It would be made out as follows:

To re-upholstering two armchairs covered in primrose yellow silk repp	£22 0s. 0d.
To repairing back of one Chippendale settee in antique crimson brocade	£15 0s. 0d.
To relaying lower steps of staircase carpet and replacing with strips of new material	£18 0s. 0d.
To patching various portions of music-room curtains in yellow velvet	£12 0s. 0d.
To supplying new silk fringes for pair of large settees	£9 0s. 0d.
To sundry scratches all over the house	£10 0s. 0d.
	£86 0s. 0d.

It may seem ungracious—even non-F—to mention such matters in public. But though eighty-six pounds would be a small sum to pay for all the pleasure which Oscar gives me, year by year, these items do mount up. And since this is a severely practical handbook, as you will have observed, the problem of pussy's claws must be faced, honestly and objectively.

The first thing to be noted is that the only chair-scratcher is Oscar. 'Four' never scratches a thing. 'Five' occasionally *assumes* the attitude of scratching, standing on his hind legs and placing his front paws firmly on a piece of new brocade. But then he pauses, turns his head, and catches one's eye. Whereupon, with an air of elaborate insouciance, he withdraws his paws, as though he had been merely smoothing out a wrinkle in the brocade. As a final proof that he thinks the whole thing grossly exaggerated, he yawns and stalks away.

But Oscar is shameless. He is a very large and very beautiful cat, with claws like sabres, and he seems positively to enjoy this supreme naughtiness. In the full light of day, under one's very nose, he will stalk over to the divan, eye it carefully, prepare to scratch, extend his claws, and drag them down. And one more scar is left on the primrose yellow silk repp, which was over two pounds a yard (single width).

Does this mean that Oscar is a sadist? Is there some obscure Jack-the-Ripper streak in him? Shall we wake up one day and see his whiskers plastered all over the front page of the *News of the World*?

No. Oscar's trouble is simply one of an unfortunate environment in his youth. It is on a par with the problems of most juvenile delinquents who have come from unsuitable homes. Unlike 'Four' and 'Five', whose early attempts at scratching were gently but firmly discouraged by giving them taps on their paws with a folded newspaper, Oscar was actually encouraged in his naughtiness. His original owner was a Chelsea artist who lived in a studio of quite exceptional squalor. Nothing was ever dusted, nothing was ever washed up, and the remains of ancient meals lingered on in odd corners for days. In this excessively Bohemian atmosphere, where most of the furniture had been purchased off pavements in Chelsea and brought home in a barrow, Oscar could scratch to his heart's content. Shouts of laughter greeted his assaults as he tore the last few pieces of sackcloth off a chair with broken springs. And bets were taken on him when he began to climb the curtains.

Then the artist decided to live abroad and Oscar, the Cockney ragamuffin, was given a new home at Merry Hall. 'What "Four" and "Five" will say I do *not* know!' observed Gaskin, in the grimmest tones. What they said will have to wait for another chapter.

Now Merry Hall was not so grand as all that, but compared with the studio it was the South Kensington Museum, the Wallace Collection, and then some. Oscar, after he had found his way around, and finished his conversations with 'Four' and 'Five'—which lasted for several days—proceeded to go about the congenial task of tearing it to pieces. At first we did not take him too seriously. 'He will soon learn,' we said optimistically, as we tapped his paws with the newspaper. 'It will not be long before he comes under the good influence of "Four" and "Five".' But he did not learn. And far from coming under the influence of 'Four' and 'Five', there were sinister signs that he might actually begin to corrupt them also. I noticed strange, frustrated gleams in their eyes as they sat and watched his forbidden activities.

What could one do? As time went on, and as more and more furniture was torn to pieces, I asked myself if there was any material which was scratch-proof. I made inquiries at various shops, and was shown several fabrics guaranteed to resist damage, but most of them looked as if they had been designed for use in homes for juvenile delinquents. Besides, I was attached to my silk repp; moreover, I had paid for it . . . heavily.

Was there anything one could spray on—any sort of deterrent? For a short while there was a period of hope. A friend brought from Paris a large box of powder which was called something like Contre-Chat. I did not much care for having such a thing about the house; the idea of being *contre-chat*, even in such an emergency, was naturally distressing. However, the situation was getting desperate; the furniture in the music-room was disintegrating before my very eyes, and we had long passed the stage where Oscar's assaults could be concealed by clipping off pieces of frayed silk with a pair of nail-scissors. And so, with some reluctance—and concealing the offend-

ing title from Oscar's interested eyes—I went into the music-room and sprinkled the powder all over Oscar's favourite pieces. I noticed, as I did so, that it had a strong scent of moth-balls. 'And now, Oscar,' I observed coldly, 'you will have to sit on the floor.' But Oscar did nothing of the sort. The powder had no effect on him. It had, however, a considerable effect on me, and even more on my friends. An overpowering scent of naphthalene is not a social asset.

Then there was the episode of the 'Scratching Tree'. This I discovered one Christmas, in the animal shop of a large London store, where I had dropped in to have a few words with an extremely beguiling macaw. The tree was a log about three feet high, mounted on a wooden base, and the young lady assured me that all cats were mad about it, and would scratch it to death, ignoring all one's 'choicer pieces' (her phrase, not mine). So I bought it and took it home, and for about twenty-four hours it was a wild success, and the choicer pieces were left in peace. Admittedly, a large log standing bolt upright next to a Queen Anne chair looked rather peculiar, but one could always put it behind a screen if anybody called. If there was not time to do so, one could pretend that one was interested in modern sculpture, and say that it was a statue of Maternity, by the new genius Catacat.

However, the charm of the Scratching Tree was short-lived. By the following evening the choicer pieces were being subjected to fresh assaults.

This was really impossible. There was only one thing to be done. I must harden my heart. Oscar's claws must be cut. The vet must be summoned without a moment's delay. I went to the telephone and lifted the receiver . . .

This, as I have observed before, is a sternly practical volume, in which no trace of whimsy must be allowed to intrude. I have hopes that it will eventually take its place on the library shelves of veterinary surgeons, who will turn to it in moments of obstetric emergency, when they are in doubt as to some detail of technique.

At the same time I must permit myself just one moment of light relief to tell you about Oscar having his claws cut.

He lay back, green-eyed, purring, stretched out on my lap. 'Pretty pussy, pretty pussy,' murmured the vet or words to that effect. Oscar raised his eyebrows. This was curiously adolescent conversation, he seemed to be saying. However . . . He extended his paw. He seemed to know all about it. There was a clip, and another clip. I held my breath. This was going far better than I had dared to hope. 'There! That's one paw done!' said the vet. But no. Oscar . . . as though he were reclining in a chair in a very grand barber's shop, yawned, drew back his paw, examined it, and extended it again. He was not satisfied. 'Dear me,' said the vet 'I have forgotten the side claw.' Whereupon Oscar emitted a faint, smug purr.

In short, Oscar actually enjoyed having his claws cut. And I believe that your cat would like having his claws cut too.

BUT . . . and I will write the word in capital letters, because it is a very big BUT . . . please remember this vital point about claw-cutting.

It should never be done at all if you live in an area where pussy is likely to encounter dogs. You will be sending him defenceless into the world. He will be unable to hit back, unable to climb to any place of refuge, and you will be guilty of the grossest cruelty.

You may ask . . . what about Oscar? Well, Oscar's area is a large country garden, surrounded by vine-clad walls and twisted hedges, and since only his front claws are cut, leaving his back ones intact, he can still scramble to safety in comparative comfort. Apart from that, there only seem to be two dogs within reasonable distance, both of them aged, corpulent and of apparently pacific dispositions. If anything large, fierce and black were suddenly to appear next door, the whole situation would have to be drastically reviewed.

Finally, let me repeat that there should never be the least need for claw-cutting if pussy has been properly brought up as a kitten. A few gentle taps with a newspaper, from time to time, should cure scratching for good and all.

E stands for Elegance.

As each year goes by the delicate word 'elegance'—so prettily shaped and with such appealing echoes—becomes more nearly obsolete, or perhaps one should say more exclusively applicable to the past. I have read, for example, a great many articles in praise of modern furniture. I have been informed that a square of orange sackcloth, supported on four hair-pin legs, with a triangular back of the same material . . . I refer, of course, to the modern chair . . . is 'exciting', 'streamlined to the contemporary trend' and 'the epitome of modern living'. All these things I can well believe, though I am not quite certain what they mean. I would merely reply, with the utmost courtesy, mumbling through my senile jaws, that if this is indeed the epitome of modern living I would greatly prefer to die.

Consider only one of the objects which are apparently regarded as essential to 'exciting', 'streamlined' modern living—the ubiquitous rubber plant. If you turn over the pages of any magazine devoted to interior decoration you will find one advertisement after another featuring this regrettable vegetable. Sometimes it is placed on the chimney piece under a reproduction of a nude by Matisse—(five guineas, including frame). Sometimes it is bang in the middle of the dining-table, which in itself is enough to give one both cramp and indigestion, being so streamlined that there is no room for one's legs, and fashioned from a peculiarly repellent variety of wood that should have been left to wilt in the jungles of Peru instead of being brought over to warp in the jungles of Peckham. Strangest of all, the rubber plant is frequently placed in the nursery, where contemporary streamlined infants are depicted playing on eye-aching rugs imported from Sweden ... I never really trusted the Swedes ... while Mummy and Daddy recline on a super-modern settee that looks as though it has been designed as a couch for a particularly evil sort of osteopath.

From these observations, which have been written with such iron restraint that my back aches, you may have gathered that I am not an admirer of modern furniture.

And you may well be asking what on earth all this has to do with cats. Just this. Cats are the most elegant of all God's creatures. As soon as a cat walks into a modern room the whole vulgar collection of 'streamlined' bits and pieces looks even more gauche and shoddy than before. Cats were created to recline on chairs by Chippendale, or perhaps one should say that chairs by Chippendale were created for cats to recline on. Their milk should be poured from jugs of Queen Anne silver, and when they walk into the garden they should do so, whenever possible, via a long and lofty Palladian colonnade, with a footman in attendance. It is bitter to realize that these simple conditions in this day and age are so seldom fulfilled.

A word about the practical application of feline elegance.

It has always struck me as extraordinary that cats are not permanently retained, at high fees, in all schools for the training of mannequins and all institutions where models are put through their paces. Before each opening of the spring and autumn collections of Paris the young women who are about to display the dresses should be gathered together, and lined up in a row, while pussy slowly parades before them, to show how it should be done. True, the models would probably all develop violent inferiority complexes, for the woman has yet to be born who can manipulate a train with the same grace as pussy twitching her tail. However, it would be worth the risk.

In particular, pussy's technique of entering a room should be studied by all women who wish to win friends and influence people.

Sometimes, on festive occasions, I have been bidden to the Savoy Hotel, which is not an eating-house I normally patronize. As I have a timid disposition and an excess of politeness I always arrive too early, and as there is a limit to the time one can spend straightening one's tie in the gentlemen's lavatory, I invariably find myself secreted behind a potted palm, looking at my wrist-watch, scanning the horizon for my hostess, and wondering when it would be safe to emerge without too much loss of caste. From this vantage-point I have had a rare opportunity to study the exits and entrances of many types

of women as they sweep up and down the staircase . . . the film stars, the American matrons, the debutantes, and that large reserve of nice women up from the country who always manage to make pink chiffon look like tweed. None of these women could hold a candle to even an alley cat in the matter of poise and deportment. For instance, none of them know how to pause. When pussy pauses, in the middle of a promenade, she automatically freezes into a posture of the utmost grace and for a moment the whole world seems to stop around her. When a woman pauses she merely looks as if something had stuck.

Consider pussy, then, all women who desire to ensnare the male. Consider her as she walks, as she sits, as she rises, as she lays herself down to sleep. You will never emulate her perfection. But with patience and humility and complete obedience to the feline laws you may at least eliminate some of your major faults.

F stands for Fur.

Before we say any more, I would like to observe, in the most dulcet tones, that though I am passionately against the institution of capital punishment, and though I have no liking for the birch as an instrument of correction, there have been moments, of recent years, when I have faintly regretted the abolition of both. These have been when I have read of the activities of the cat thieves. When I think of those sub-human brutes, prowling round the dark alleys, thrusting out a thieving arm to grip somebody's pet round the throat . . . when I think of the sack, the struggles, the terror, the suffocation . . . but then, I try not to think of these things, which is weak of me. For if some people had not the courage to endure the torture of thinking of them, there would never be any action.

However, these were meant to be happy pages, so we will send these brutes skulking back into the shadows, with the hope that there may be some special corner of hell reserved for them, in which they will be tied up in sacks, slowly suffocated, and finally skinned to the accompaniment of the Hallelujah Chorus sung by a massed choir of Siamese kittens.

And now for a few thoughts on fur.

At the risk of causing dissension, I must confess that the most *de luxe* form of feline fur, the Persian, is not the variety which affords me, personally, the greatest delight. I see its beauty, I appreciate its miraculous sheen and delicacy, and I need hardly say that when a Persian cat enters the room, with all the glamorous assurance of a film star, I hastily straighten my tie and smooth my hair and click my heels. That is really the trouble—for me—about Persians and their fur. I cannot relax with them. Even when they lie on their backs and demand tummy-rubbing, I feel that I should be taking a liberty if I obeyed their commands—rather as though a glittering prima donna were to sink on to a rich divan, indicating that a moment's dalliance might not be unacceptable. Would not one get all tangled up with tiaras and ostrich-feather capes? I ask only for information;

such a situation has not yet arisen in my life, and becomes daily more improbable.

Again, I get worried about fur in the tummy. Not fur in *my* tummy, but in the Persian's. I seem to remember, from the distant past, tales of Persians who had to have balls of fur extracted from them. Then there is the question of lumpiness. Whenever you stroke a Persian—always with this peculiar feeling that you are taking liberties with a prima donna—you come across these lumps. Do they disturb the Persian? Do they keep it awake at nights? Are they being properly attended to? Is some slave with a silver comb perpetually in attendance, with a mirror and a bowl of cream? The answer, in these days of the Welfare State, is probably in the negative. All the best slaves, who ought to be ministering to Persian cats, are almost certainly in the employment of the London County Council, ministering to a lot of nasty little boys and girls.

For this curious complex of reasons, therefore, I have never owned a Persian cat. Or perhaps it would be more fitting to say that I have never been owned by one.

Some cats, as we all know, are born in full evening dress. White shirt, white tie . . . (whiskers) . . . black tails and all. The illusion is perfect, particularly when they also have smart black paws to match. I love cats in evening dress; they wear it so much more elegantly than we do. Moreover, they never look incongruous in it. There are very few young men who can sit on a wall in Chelsea, at nine o'clock in the morning, in deep evening dress, delicately scratching their ears, without exciting adverse comment. Indeed, I only knew one, and he came to a bad end. But a great many cats can do it, and always with grace.

Perhaps the most sheerly beautiful of all feline furs is worn by the Siamese. I suppose one would call it beige, but beige has always seemed to me a rather common word, possibly because I knew a very common Australian woman who was always wandering about people's houses, unasked, and telling them that they should have their walls painted beige. She pronounced it 'beeyige' and she made it sound like a sort of cheese. One can't really catalogue the fur of a Siamese; sometimes it is corn-colour, flecked with gold, at others it is old ivory, and there are some very soigné and quite alarmingly distinguished blue points who look as if they had stepped straight out of Lanvin's, who I still think makes the prettiest clothes, whatever anybody may say. And then, of course, the beauty of the Siamese fur is not exactly diminished by the fact that it is always offset by those marvellous brown gloves, those superb stockings, and finally . . . the jewels of the eyes, which are sapphire or aquamarine or stained-glass-window, according to age and breeding and temperament.

But really it is rather churlish to set one fur against another. There are candle-lit evenings when the fur of my own 'Four' is jet, with a sheen of electric blue; he is the blackest of black pussies but after you have been stroking him for some time this curious and strangely beautiful shade of blue flickers over his back.

And then—what about the fur of tabbies, which affords one of the many proofs that Nature has a sense of humour? My own 'Five' has a smudge on his nose which compels one to think of him as a low comedian. This leads to all sorts of emotional complications.

For there are times when 'Five' does not feel in the least like a low comedian, times when he is frightened or bewildered or filled with a nameless *malaise*, times when he is simply sentimental. Whereupon he comes and sits by one's chair and gazes up with those immense green eyes, and one looks down at him with every intention of being emotionally co-operative and adjusting oneself to his mood. But always there is that smudge on the nose and really it is extremely difficult, unless one is a brilliant actor, not to smile at it. Which, of course, would be quite shattering for 'Five', because he would feel that one was making fun of him.

And that leads to yet another reflection. It has nothing to do with F for Fur, but I will set it down while it occurs to me. I am quite certain that all animals who have been domesticated are intensely sensitive to ridicule and sarcasm. To cats ... maybe even more to dogs ... a sneer or a guffaw can be more wounding than a blow. It is a bitter reminder of their 'inferior' status; it sends them back to the darkness of the jungle from which we have taken them.

Not for the first time, I feel thankful that 'Five' cannot read. If he could, and if he chanced upon these pages, I should never be able to look him in the face again.

G stands for Gardening.

All cats are keen gardeners, and in every garden that I have ever made, their shadows lie across the path. Sometimes, I must admit, the garden might have been made more easily without their assistance. Indeed, whenever I think of cats and gardens, I am reminded of the affectionate dedication in one of Mr P. G. Wodehouse's novels . . . 'To my dear daughter Leonora, without whose constant advice and encouragement, this book would have been finished in half the time.'

Like their owners, cats soon decide which form of gardening most appeals to them—though none of them, alas, ever takes any interest in weeding. All of them, however, are keen waterers; indeed, they co-operate in this task with such enthusiasm that they lend it an air of drama with which it is not usually associated. If one is using the hose, and if the hose has a leak where it fits on to the tap—and I have yet to meet the hose which has not—pussy feels obliged to investigate this phenomenon, to stalk round it, to put out a tentative paw at the dripping water, to prod it, to frisk round it, and generally to make one feel that something very exciting is occurring—as, of course, it is. When the hose is in action, the drama rises to fresh heights, with pussy lurking behind shrubs (usually in the precise place where one wishes to direct the water) and giving a brilliant histrionic display of alarm. Sometimes, on these occasions, I close my eyes for a moment and try to enter into pussy's mind and I think I can dimly realize how she is feeling. Think of it! One is lurking under a giant tree and across the sky an immense stream of silver is streaking like some fantastic water-spout; there are sounds of thunder as it splashes on the giant leaves and strikes the parched earth; and always there is the shadow of a two-legged monster above one, the Genie of the Waters.

Watering with the can is less emotionally exhausting; indeed I can think of few diversions more soothing, more restful to the soul, than an hour spent in this fashion, on a warm summer evening in an old country garden with a cat in attendance. The fragrance that rises from the grateful earth is like a benison; there is a subtle, shadowy beauty in the darkening soil, a ghostly music in the soft hiss and gurgle of the water. And always of course there is pussy, watching and waiting. There are times, on very hot evenings, when it is permissible to switch the can so that for a second a few drops of water fall across pussy's back. This allows her an opportunity to give a fine display of outraged indignation which leads, in its turn, to a very pleasant scene of reconciliation, with pussy lurking coyly in an inaccessible position under a prickly berberis, while one muddies one's trousers and scratches one's hands trying to coax her out.

There are times—even the most earnest of Fs must admit this—when pussy's gardening activities are more of a hindrance than a help. For example, when seeds have been sown in the open ground, it is discouraging to look out of the window and see that pussy is using the precise place where they are sown as a public convenience. A nice new seed-bed, to pussy, is an immediate reminder that the time has come for washing the hands or powdering the nose; it is almost as though one had stuck a little label into the earth with the world 'Toilette' written in bold black letters.

I really do not quite know how one deals with this problem. No great purpose is served by rushing across the lawn, shooing and clapping one's hands; such a procedure is unfair to pussy and unduly agitating to one's own pulse; besides, by the time one has reached the seed-bed it is probably too late, and one's shilling packet of love-in-the-mist or clarkia or candytuft is scattered to the four winds. One can, of course, protect the seeds with a cloche, but I never much care for cloches in a garden; they are always getting broken and spattered with mud, and they set one's teeth on edge with the noise they make when their edges grate together. Perhaps the best plan is to adopt the same procedure as we use to keep sparrows off crocuses, i.e. to cover the seed bed with a network of black cotton attached to twigs. Even this, however, is not entirely satisfactory, particularly if kittens are around. They have a habit of treating the cotton as though it were a maze specially designed for their own amusement. After a long experience of cats and gardens I have decided that the wisest and cheapest thing to do is to forget about seeds and buy boxes of seedlings.

There should be no need, one hopes, to remind the experienced F of the dangers which may lie waiting for cats in gardens where such things as weed killers are used. And yet, when I think of my own shortcomings in this respect, I feel that a word of warning would not be out of place.

Never, as long as I live, will I forget the awful drama of 'One', the Scotch firs, and the nicotine powder. I had planted a coppice of Scotch firs, at the end of the orchard at Merry Hall. If you have never planted Scotch firs you might be pardoned for thinking that they were a fairly simple tree to grow. They are not. They always develop—at least, mine do—a horrible little bug at the tip of the new growth, which burrows into the tender skin and eventually kills it. This means the loss of a year's growth.

What to do? At first, I used to go round every tree, search out the bugs, and gouge them to death by impaling them with the sharp end of a twig. This was (*a*) exhausting and (*b*) stomach-turning, because the bugs, when gouged, turned into a peculiarly repellent form of yellow custard. Then I began to experiment with various sprays, none of which had the least effect. At last, I discovered nicotine powder. One applied it by means of a thing that looked like an attenuated concertina, which produced clouds of acrid dust, when shaken. This completely devastated the bugs, and the pine trees shot up, straight and green and immaculate.

But I had not realized that nicotine powder was a deadly poison and in the second year I was filled with feelings of such loathing for the bugs—who had started all over again—that I used it in quite inordinate quantities, so that a lot of it spattered the grass below. And that was how 'One' picked it up, and sampled it with his pink tongue, and felt the pangs of death inside him. Never shall I forget seeing him staggering towards me across the lawn, his eyes glazed, his body twisted with pain. This is a beastly memory, and I won't dwell on the twenty-four hours which ensued, where 'One' lay moaning in a dark cupboard. The only reason why I recall the episode is to remind Fs, if ever they should have recourse to poison, to use it with the utmost discretion. Better still, not to use it at all.

Apart from this one exception, all my memories of cats and gardens are ringed with happiness. At random I recall the blue of 'One's' eyes reflecting the blue of the tall clusters of anchusas under which he used to dispose himself on hot summer afternoons. I would wander out to the herbaceous border—probably for the twentieth time during the day—and see the anchusas looking faintly disturbed, and step softly over the parched earth, and find him there in the cool green shade that was starred with the miraculous blue of the flowers. I would speak to him, and the sleepy eyes would open, and two blues would melt together . . . and I would feel that this was one of those moments of peace and beauty which made up for all the struggles and heartaches of life.

H stands for History.

This letter should really be dedicated to Christabel[1] for without her classic *Dictionary of Cat-Lovers* it could not have been compiled. Never was there a wiser, more seductive anthology, in which the erudition is worn as lightly as a feather drifting past the wondering eyes of a kitten. It seems difficult to believe that the inspiration for this work, which is curiously feminine in spite of the weight of its scholarship, came at one of the most sombre moments of the war, in a darkened train, while an 'Alert' was sounding. A fellow passenger observed that the sound of the sirens was 'like the screaming of demon cats in agony'. This unknown traveller proved, in subsequent conversation, to be F. Sitting next to him was a militant non-F. The other occupants of the carriage were F and semi-F. They talked, they argued, the train rattled on through the mysterious blackness of the countryside; Christabel sat in a corner and thought her thoughts. And that was how it all began.

With a few of the facts in this dictionary I was already familiar; whenever I have been reading history, the appearance of a cat on the stage, even for a fleeting moment, has been enough to fix the event in my memory for ever. (I have often regretted that cats played

[1] The Dowager Lady Aberconway.

no part in the interminable religious squabbles of the sixteenth century; a few brisk tabbies, waltzing through the Thirty-Nine Articles, might have given those arid paragraphs a semblance of interest.) And cats *have* made a great many appearances on the world's stage, often in the most distinguished company. One of the most persistent legends of the East concerns the prophet Mahomet who so greatly loved his cat that once, when it was sleeping by his side, he cut off the sleeve of his robe rather than disturb it. Here indeed was a master F, and one could only wish that the modern inhabitants of the Arab countries, who are not noticeably kind to animals, had taken his lesson to heart.

All the true Fs at some time or other have emulated Mahomet's example . . . not perhaps so drastically as to cut off portions of their attire, but enough to put themselves to considerable inconvenience. Such a one was President Theodore Roosevelt, whose term of office, though marked by other events of minor importance, was particularly memorable because of the role played by Slippers, the White House Cat. Slippers was grey, and he had six toes on each foot which

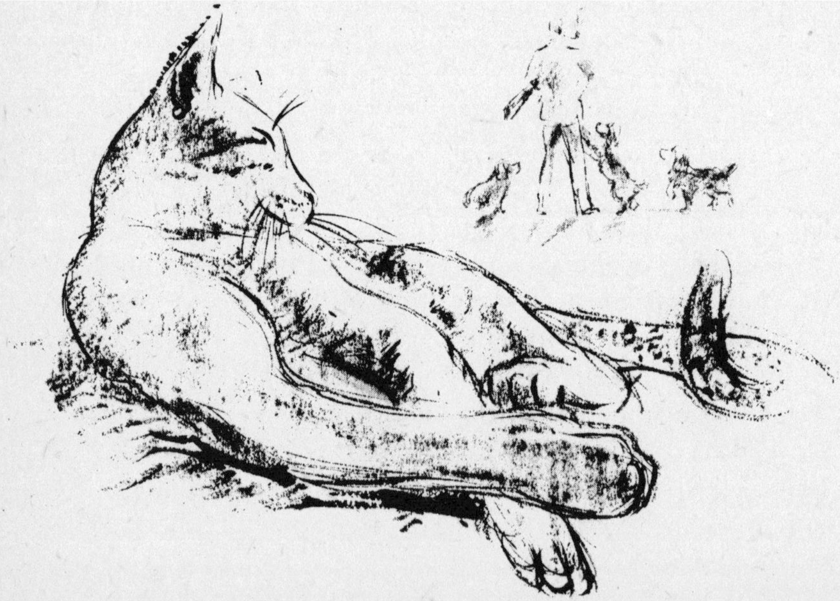

earned him his curious name. My favourite story about him concerns a very grand diplomatic dinner party where he lay on his back in the middle of a narrow corridor down which the President and his guests had to make their way. It was a glittering procession of ambassadors and ambassadresses, but Slippers quite rightly took precedence over all of them. Rather than disturb him the President bowed low, and steered his ambassadress to one side. (She was not amused, for she was noticeably non-F.) 'Whereupon', writes the chronicler, 'the representatives of Great Britain and of France, of Germany and Italy, of all the empires and of the little kingdoms, followed suit, paying their respects to Slippers quite as effectually as if the warships of their nations had thundered out a salute.' Which, of course, is how it should be.

The above story has been quoted fairly frequently, but there is one—even more remarkable because it concerns George Washington—which I have never seen in print. Apparently Washington was so eminently F that at Mount Vernon he actually made a cat-door for his own cat with his own hands—an ingenious little contrivance leading from the study to the garden. Moreover, this door can be seen by tourists to this day. This, surely, is the most important news; it is also yet another example of the strange obtuseness of the historians. For though I have been conducted more than once round Mount Vernon, and been regaled at length with quantities of details about Washington's career, nobody ever dreamt of pointing to the most important relic in the house . . . the cat-door. Nor, as far as I can recall, have any historians mentioned that Washington was F at all. They prefer to inform us that he never told a lie—an omission which, one would have thought, it would have been kinder to hush up.

Quite evidently, the creation of cat-doors is the mark of a noble mind, and a lofty spirit of independence which cherishes freedom not only for man but for beast. One of the most illustrious cat-doors recorded in history was cut by the great Isaac Newton; indeed, he cut two of them, one large hole for his cat, and one small hole for her kitten. This fact might be borne in mind by Fs who occasionally engage in arguments with non-Fs.

I suggested above that even the Thirty-Nine Articles might have been enlivened by a little feline diversion. This did in fact once occur, in the House of Commons, or something very like it. In July of the year 1874 there was a debate on the Public Worship Regulation Bill. It was a boring subject, expounded by a very boring man, Sir William Harcourt, in the presence of the supreme bore of all time, Mr Gladstone. Suddenly an immense grey tabby cat stalked grandly down the opposition gangway, turned its head, took one look at Sir William Harcourt, registered disgust . . . Harcourt was obviously non-F . . . and shot out of the House, over the shoulders of the members sitting on the front Ministerial bench.

Perhaps it is because of their own fierce love of freedom that cats have always shown a strange sympathy for prisoners. One of these was Henry Wriothesly, third Earl of Southampton, the friend of

Shakespeare and one of the posthumous contestants for the role of 'onlie begetter' of the sonnets. Well, he seems as likely a candidate as any of the others, particularly after one has studied the portrait of him at Welbeck. This shows a young man with wide, dreaming eyes, pale delicate hands, and in the background a most beguiling cat, glossy and relaxed and evidently well tended. When Southampton married, he incurred the disfavour of Elizabeth—who was, of course, blatantly non-F. He was sentenced to solitary confinement for life, in the Tower. This was too much for his favourite cat, who found its way to the Tower and climbed down the chimney into his apartment where, so the legend goes, it stayed with him to the end. This is one of the pleasantest examples of the fact that a cat can not only look at a Queen, but can flout her authority.

But the most celebrated case of a cat who cared for a prisoner is afforded by Sir Henry Wyatt in the fifteenth century. Because of his loyalty to the Lancastrian party, Richard III threw him in one of his foulest prisons 'where hee had neither bed to lie on, nor cloaths sufficient to warme him, nor meate for his mouth'. And while he lay there in these dreadful circumstances, a cat—realizing that a true F was in great distress—made her way into the dungeon and offered her services. 'And after this, shee would come every day unto him, divers times, and when shee could gett one, bring him a pigeon.'

This pigeon, to the non-F, may sound like a 'property' bird. But the legend, not only to the F but to the historian, has the ring of truth, and it is reinforced by a strangely moving contemporary portrait of Wyatt, in his later years, sitting in prison beside his cat, who is gazing at him in adoration and at the same time somewhat incongruously manipulating a pigeon through the bars of the cell.

I have indicated, very briefly, a few of the roles which cats have played in history. Lest I should be accused of undue partiality, let us end with the story of the Empress Wu. (It is conceivable that some people may have forgotten that the Empress Wu was the protégée of the Empress Wang, whom she eventually supplanted in the year 683. However, every schoolboy knows that the Empress Wang ... or was it Wong? ... was hostile to the concubine Hsiao who was the favourite of the Emperor T'ai Tsung. One almost blushes to remind the reader that Wu married the Emperor Kao Tsung. Anyway, to cut a long story short, in more senses than one, Wu eventually chopped off everybody's hands and feet, Wang's, Wong's, T'ai Tsung's, Kao Tsung's and Uncle Tom Cobley's and all.)

Wu was unabashedly F. One says this with a certain diffidence, for she would seem, at this distance, to have had a strain of ruthlessness in her character. And yet, how are we to know whether Wang—or Wong—and T'ai Tsung and Kao Tsung were not even more ruthless? Be that as it may, Wu had some very modern ideas. She was extremely worried about the warring sects of her empire, and she was anxious to unite them in one great peaceful federation. So she decided to set them an example. With the assistance of her official censor P'eng-Hsien-Chueh (that will be the last one) she trained her cat, whose name is fortunately lost in the mists of time, to eat off the same plate as her parrot. A great Exhibition was staged, to show this amiable phenomenon to the warring chieftains. Unfortunately something went wrong; the anonymous pussy was hungry. So it bit off the parrot's head and ate it.

History records that the Empress was 'very much embarrassed'. One's own reaction is that even cats, in off moments, will behave very much like members of the United Nations.

J stands for Inventions.

I have always regretted that cats cannot be provided with latchkeys. However domesticated they may appear to be, they are wild creatures at heart, and as the darkness falls they hear the call of the jungle. True, the jungle may be only a backyard, and the tropical undergrowth may be confined to a speckled laurel and a cluster of bedraggled ivy. But at least it is in the open air, and under the stars, and the night wind is tingling with a thousand mysterious scents. And the wall can be leapt upon, and stalked along, and transformed into a magic thoroughfare.

To keep a cat indoors, night after night, with nothing to do but to stare at this dark paradise through a pane of glass, and lash its tail impotently against the net curtains, seems to me grossly inconsiderate, if not actually cruel. If I myself had been a cat in the days of the Regency—and I have sober reasons for believing this to have been the case—I should have described it as 'the outside of enough'.

Hence my invention of the cat-door. I call it 'my' invention, for though Newton, as we have seen, thought of it first, I thought of it long before I knew that Newton had thought about it. However, no true F would wish to claim exclusive rights in so beneficent an invention, still less to patent it. On the contrary, I would like to see more and more cat-doors, bigger and better cat-doors, appearing all over the country. I would like the electorate to become cat-door-conscious, and if I were on the London County Council I would vote for cat-doors to be made compulsory on all new building estates, with a high priority over such inessentials as damp-courses and fire escapes.

The making of a cat-door can be very simply described. All you have to do is to cut out a square of wood near the base of one of the doors in your house. Most people will probably choose the door of the kitchen. Then you cut an inch off the bottom of the square of wood and refix by means of a pair of pivots. It will then swing backwards and forwards quite easily.

I should perhaps warn you that in spite of the naked simplicity of this device, the average carpenter will approach it with mistrust, indeed with trepidation. There will be a great deal of argument about it. But eventually, if he perseveres, the true F will wear the carpenter down.

I have two cat-doors in my own house; one of them leads from the kitchen down a flight of steps into a little courtyard; the other leads straight from the music-room on to the open lawn. The gentle sound of the doors swinging backwards and forwards at all times of the day and the night, is a pleasing accompaniment to my life; it reminds me that the cats are alert and fully occupied and intent upon their many tasks of inspection, espionage and sentry work. Often, when I have been feeling lonely, when a book has been thrust aside in boredom, when the keys of the piano, softly lit, hold no invitation to the dance, I have lain back and stared at the shadows on the ceiling, wondering what life is all about ... and then, suddenly, there is the echo of the swinging door, and across the carpet, walking with the utmost delicacy and precision, stalks 'Four' or 'Five' or Oscar. Whichever it may be, his tail is always very upright, and as he walks he talks ... small, friendly, feline talk, delivered in the softest of mews ... mews which melt into purrs as he approaches the sofa. He sits down on the floor beside me, regarding my long legs, my old jumper, and my floppy arms, with a purely practical interest. Which part of this large male body will form the most appropriate lap? Usually he settles for the chest. Whereupon he springs up and there is a feeling of cold fur—for the night is frosty—and the tip of an icy nose, thrust against my wrist and a positive tattoo of purrs. And I no longer wonder what life is all about.

Some very spoiled cats, after a while, develop a habit of sitting in front of the cat-door with an air of profound pathos, pretending that they do not understand how to get through it. They peer through the little gap at the bottom, they heave profound sighs, they gaze up with anguished expressions, pleading that the door may be opened for them in the ordinary way.

When this happens, the owner must be ruthless. He must steel his heart. The cat knows perfectly well how to go through the cat-door; it has gone through at least a thousand times; and this sudden reluctance to use it is simply an 'act'. It is merely doing it to annoy, because it knows it teases. The owner must not allow himself to be blackmailed in this manner. In no circumstances must he open the door. His best plan is to be quite nonchalant. A little light-hearted conversation about the weather ... a swift, delicate stroke ... a few bars, hummed quite casually, of a popular tune. He must not allow the atmosphere to grow too tense. Otherwise he will gradually be hypnotized by those appealing eyes, and he will find himself opening the door, willy-nilly.

With kittens, on their first introduction to the door, his technique will of course be very different. He should first swing the door gently backwards and forwards in order to make the kitten familiar with its movement. Then, for a few moments, he should hold the door open, extended outwards, so that the kitten may be assured that there is nothing sinister on the other side. After which he should lift the kitten with great firmness, press its paws against the door, and push it through. This action may possibly be resented by the kitten, who will dart away under the nearest rhododendron, and refuse to be coaxed inside until it has caused the maximum of trouble. But little by little the kitten will accustom itself to the door, and use it as a matter of course.

To sum up, Fs who have not equipped themselves with cat-doors should give the matter their early and earnest consideration. True, they may be meticulous about leaving the kitchen window open. They may have evolved the most elaborate technique about letting pussy out at night, and tapping plates with a fork to get her back again. But these are merely makeshifts. Without a cat-door the owner of a house is living, from an F point of view, in the Middle Ages.

J stands for Journeys.

At some time or other of their lives nearly all Fs—and quite a large number of non-Fs—have had the scarifying experience of transporting pussy, by car or by rail, to a new home. The word 'scarifying' is bracketed in *Roget's Thesaurus* with such words as 'crushing', 'harrowing', 'torturing', 'agonizing' and 'excruciating'. There are also cross-references to 'daggers in the breast' and 'thorns in the side'. For the purposes of this section of our alphabet all these expressions are strictly apposite.

Perhaps the most 'scarifying'—or, to revert to Roget, 'pothering', 'corroding' and altogether 'wherreting'—experience I ever had of cat transport was during the war, when I was obliged to drive no less than five Siamese cats to a safe area all the way from London to Devonshire. It had to be done on the spur of the moment, after a night of fire-watching, through smoking streets that were railed off with the sinister sign 'Unexploded Bomb'. As I drove, the wail of the sirens blended in a sort of infernal harmony with the wail of the Siamese cats, who were struggling in baskets which were far too small for them. I was alone, I had no time to stop and comfort them, and by the journey's end I was even nearer to nervous collapse than the cats themselves. And though I love the wail of a Siamese, there are times when, for a fleeting second, it still strikes a chill to my heart.

Happily, most of the journeys we take with cats are less wherreting. However, they are quite wherreting enough. Here, therefore, are a few hints which—though they will seem trite to the expert Fs—may perhaps be of value to less experienced persons.

Let us assume that only one pussy is to be transported—a simple, uncomplicated pussy of some three summers—and that the journey involves a short trip by motor car and a longer trip by train. The first question to be answered is ... what shall we carry her in? By far the most satisfactory conveyance, in my experience, is a linen basket, which allows plenty of air, and enough, but not too much, light. The basket should of course be lined with something soft, ideally a rug or a blanket on which pussy has been accustomed to sleep.

We will draw a veil over the painful process of putting pussy into the basket, lifting her into the car, and carrying her through the frightening racket of the station. There are no particular technical difficulties involved in these procedures, all that is needed is a kind heart, a sound stomach, nerves of steel, and a hide of brass ... the latter in order to enable one to face the outraged looks of one's travelling companions, who invariably assume, from the piercing wails that come from the basket, that one is some exceptionally degraded type of cat-torturer.

Now comes a point of exceptional importance.

Whatever else you may do, never let pussy out of the basket.

The wails may rise to agonizing heights, they may be charged with bitter reproach and desperate entreaty, but you must harden your heart. This is one of those occasions when you really must 'be cruel to be kind'. (That is a phrase I have never greatly cared for; it has a nasty echo of 'spare the rod and spoil the child'. I suspect that there are occasions when the cruel-to-be-kind fraternity secretly enjoy the act of cruelty.)

But surely, this is an occasion when the phrase rings true. For which is the greater cruelty ... to keep pussy in the basket, or to let her out? In the basket, admittedly, she is cramped, but she is not actually in pain. She has plenty of air. She is not in the dark. And though the whole situation is strange and frightening, at least she has a familiar voice to comfort her, and a familiar finger to scratch her head.

But if she is let out she immediately leaps into a world of sheer terror, a world of blinding lights and darting shadows, speeding by at sixty miles per hour. She can have only one impulse in her wildly beating heart, to escape . . . anyhow, anywhere, at any cost, back to the quiet world from which you have so recently dragged her. And escape, unless you are very careful, she will. A cat in these circumstances is endowed with the strength of a fiend, and even a small Siamese kitten is a full-time job.

We have observed, time and again, that this is intended to be a sternly practical book. A book in which the prose gives pride of place to the precept. A book destined for the dusty shelves of veterinary surgeons, where it will stand next to such volumes as *Cows—their Cause and Cure*. Why it should so often be necessary to remind myself of

this patent fact I find it hard to say; perhaps it is because 'Five' has been so constantly perched on the desk beside me, giving a playful dab to my pen.

Whatever the reason, we will now substantiate our claim.

For this is where we invoke the aid of science, in the shape of a mild, soothing pill, with 'Four', 'Five' and Oscar as examples of its efficacy.

Before doing so, however, it is only fair to point out that 'Four', 'Five' and Oscar may perhaps be regarded as somewhat exceptional felines. They have enjoyed a superior education. They have a wide and cosmopolitan circle of human acquaintances. Moreover, they have been accustomed to publicity. They have not sought it, but it has been thrust upon them. They are fully accustomed to being lifted from repose and seated upon chairs in the music-room in order to pose for young gentlemen who stand before them and flash bulbs at them. True, they seldom pose for long. Indeed, one flash is usually enough to send them scurrying out through the cat-door into the garden, from which I refuse to rescue them, because I do not wish them to be subjected to too much nervous strain. All the same, I believe they rather like publicity, in their secret hearts. Every Christmas I prepare a little cat calendar which has a modest sale in the F world. This has a photograph of a cat for every month, with a few words from myself underneath each photograph. Nearly always I manage to squeeze in a picture of 'Four', 'Five' and Oscar. But last year 'Five' had to be left out, and was supplanted by a Siamese kitten, of exceptional allurement, dabbing at a spray of pear-blossom. When the calendar was placed on Gaskin's mantelpiece, a few days before Christmas, 'Five' took one look at it, registered acute disgust, and stalked out into the garden in a fit of sulks.

Back to science and the soothing pill. 'Surely,' the reader may ask, 'there can be no need of soporifics with cats who are so used to the bright lights? Surely they would face the sternest of ordeals with equanimity, and display their habitual sang-froid even if they were obliged to ride through London in the Lord Mayor's coach?' This is not the case. My cats, when they feel like it, can be as temperamental as anybody else's. Every Tuesday morning, for instance, at approximately ten o'clock, the whole household is disorganized by cats shooting violently in all directions, in a state of the greatest alarm. Oscar rushes to a cupboard, 'Five' leaps on to a tallboy, 'Four' squeezes under Gaskin's bed. The cause of all this commotion is an agreeable young dustman, going his weekly round. All he has done is to bang the lids of the dustbins. Moreover—as I have gathered from casual conversation—he is a highly civilized person, who spends his dustman's money on long-playing records of Khachaturian. (Which may account for the vigour with which he percusses the lids.) In spite of this, as far as 'Four', 'Five' and Oscar are concerned, he might be a fiend incarnate, clanging them to hell.

I repeat, my cats are just as temperamental as yours. And yet, a single little pill enabled them to make the journey from Merry Hall to Richmond with complete tranquillity. They were not transported, they were wafted. They yawned, they disposed themselves in the baskets, they curled themselves up, and if they had been confined to the use of the English language, they would have murmured ... 'Home Charles, and avoid the Kingston by-pass.'

I do not know the name of the pill. But any good vet., surely, will know about it, and be able to instruct you in its use. It does not actually send pussy to sleep, and it does not entirely prevent an occasional faint mew of protest from the inside of the basket. But it is a mew that ends in a yawn, and the yawning seems to persist, in lessening degrees, for about forty-eight hours. By when, let us hope, pussy will be firmly re-established and her new life will have begun.

K stands for Kneading.

This refers, of course, to the charming alternating movement of the front paws made by pussy in moments of great contentment. First one paw is raised and then the other, with the utmost grace; the claws are slightly but amiably protruded; sometimes the eyes are narrowed. This is evidently an hour when all is right with the world.

I have sometimes thought that this delightful accomplishment might be renamed 'Organ-Playing'. This demands a word of explanation. Occasionally, in order to enter more closely into the minds of cats, I have endeavoured to copy their physical habits. I am past the age of rushing up the trunks of apple trees or for skidding down them. ('Skidding' is, I think, the right word with which to describe the action of a cat descending the trunk of a tree. They never seem quite happy about it. I am sure that all Fs will have shared with me those moments of agonized apprehension when one has stood at the foot of a tall tree . . . usually at dusk in a high wind . . . trying to coax some foolhardy creature back to earth. This is one of the few occasions when cats seem to lose their heads. Below them stretches the nice broad, solid trunk of the tree, waiting to conduct them to safety. At the bottom of the trunk stands their master, making the most ingratiating noises, and—in cases of extremity—tapping a plate of fish. But they pay no heed. Just when one thinks that they are near enough to be reached by a ladder, off they dart down some truant branch, and sway and stagger and balance in the wind, making the most piteous noises.)

But all this is taking us away from the matter under discussion—organ-playing. As I was saying, there are days when I try to enter into the feline mind by emulating their physical habits. It was my cat 'Five' who gave me my first organ lesson, one day when I was lying in bed. Until that morning I had always regarded this movement as 'kneading'. 'Five' was looking at me with a very intent expression, as though he were challenging me to a kneading competition. 'Very well,' I said to him, 'if you desire me to knead, I will knead. It will be a useful Yogi exercise in tranquillity and spiritual elevation.' So I pushed aside an extremely brutal issue of *Life*, filled with photographs of corpses stretched on beaches in Malaya, and began . . . tentatively . . . to 'knead'. I say 'tentatively' because an amateur is always embarrassed in the presence of a professional. And then, all of a sudden, I forgot 'Five' and his green, appraising eyes, for I realized that I was inadvertently playing the slow movement of Bach's Italian Concerto on the blanket. The melody, slightly muffled in wool, was unmistakable, the bass—faintly entangled in the sheets—was adequate. As I continued to 'knead' I found myself pulling out invisible stops—here a vox humana, there a cor anglais or a tremolo.

Try it for yourself, and you will see what I mean.

All my three cats are expert organists, but their techniques vary greatly and their repertoires are quite different. 'Five' specializes in quiet chorales, 'Four' in Bach fugues. The most spectacular player is Oscar, whose favourite composer is evidently Mahler. When Oscar leaps on to my bed, to give a recital, his paws pound the blankets—which are of the cellular variety—with such frenzy that small skeins of wool are detached. A tremendous bass purr echoes from the depths of his white chest, and the eyes are half closed in ecstasy. It is a moving and impressive performance, which has only one drawback. So exalted does Oscar become that he is inclined to dribble.

A simple solution to this problem will be found in the chapter devoted to Purring.

There is an infinite variety of techniques in feline organ-playing. To me, one of the most charming is when pussy is sitting at one's feet, and gazing up at one, and—because her mood is amiable and the sun is shining—she very lightly touches the keys, as it were, with one paw. Only Fs will realize that she is playing the organ at all, for this is indeed the most subtle and elusive form of feline music.

Pussy may sometimes decide to play the organ in circumstances inconvenient to her master, for example, on his knees. This frequently occurs during the watching of television. Pussy, observing a lap—for even gentlemen, if properly trained, are capable of forming laps—will spring up, curl around, face the screen, purr, and begin to run her paws lightly over the keyboard, in other words, to dig her claws into the owner's knees.

This is a moment when all Fs have an opportunity of proving their quality. Non-Fs, needless to say, will immediately push pussy off their laps with some crude and vulgar expletive, and if they are of an exceptionally beastly disposition, they will give pussy a slap.

But the true F will grin and bear it. If the organ-playing becomes particularly passionate he can comfort himself with the thought that there is probably some iodine in the bathroom.

L stands for going to the Loo.

This section might also have come under P for Powdering the Nose, or W for Washing the Hands. It should be skipped by persons of excessive sensibility.

To all true Fs the feline routine of going to the Loo, particularly if the Loo is situated in a large garden, and not too near the seedlings, is an elegant and entirely inoffensive performance . . . which is more than can be said for similar operations by members of the human race.

It is also, for me at any rate, a mysterious and somewhat awe-inspiring spectacle. From what distant ages were those intricate techniques handed down? From what ancient volume of etiquette has the smallest kitten learned how to behave, as it totters on to its box of sand and gives its first feeble scrape with the left paw? (Kittens always start with the *left* paw . . . a fact which I should have brought to the attention of Mr Darwin if I had been honoured with his friendship. In later life they use either paw indiscriminately.)

The whole thing is as formal and as stately as a minuet. Pussy walks across the lawn, to go to the Loo. Which, of the myriad loos at her disposal, shall she choose? The seedling bed, needless to say, would be ideal, but she recalls that the last time she used it there was a most ridiculous commotion. Perhaps it had better be the kitchen garden, where humans are not so fussy. So off she goes, and finds a very pleasing loo in the shape of a patch of newly dug earth. Out comes her paw ... and then, unaccountably, she changes her mind. A superior loo, about ten feet away, has suggested itself. But no ... the first one was better. So back she goes. One paw comes out again, and scrapes and scrapes (always one paw at a time) ... and then the other, till all is in readiness. And then, the act. Very still, head erect, shoulders back. Like a statue from the era of Tutankhamen. A wild creature, performing an essential function, with the utmost dignity and distinction.

The post-operative technique, to use a piece of jargon from the surgical ward, is not without its interest. In the interests of feline hygiene there must be more scraping, to conceal any displeasing evidence of what has occurred. But the scraping seems to go to pussy's head. Even after the hygienic necessities have been observed there will be more scrapings, apparently at random, first with one paw, then with the other paw, with the sweet earth shooting out in all directions.

Indeed, it would seem that the very act of going to the loo, or rather, of having gone to the loo, produces in pussy a feeling of inexplicable exhilaration. Consider one of my own cats, 'Four', whose favourite loo is situated on the rhododendron bank. As soon as the last delicate sweep has scattered the last fragment of earth, there is a dramatic pause, in which he stares around him in wild surmise. And then, suddenly, he shoots across the lawn towards the house at lightning speed, bound upon bound, whiskers flying in the wind, tail as erect as a pennant ... a streamlined symbol of delight.

I have often thought how interesting it would be if this conduct were general among human beings. Suppose that one were walking down the corridor of a French hotel, past the door marked 'Dames'. Suppose that the door were suddenly to be flung open, revealing a lady who stood in the entrance, clasping her hands and gazing around her with starry eyes and parted lips. And suppose that she were then to break into peals of girlish laughter and rush down the corridor, screaming 'Je sors de la toilette, je sors de la toilette délicieuse!' One would be enthralled. This is yet another example of the fact that females have much to learn from felines.

In an emergency, pussy will go to the utmost trouble in order to keep up her high standard of cleanliness. Normally, of course, if she wishes to 'leave the room', she walks with calm dignity to the door, looks over her shoulder, and waits for the door to be opened. But if she is shut up alone in a house where there is no means of exit, without even a box for her convenience, and if she is unable to wait any longer, she usually seeks high and low for some place where she will cause the minimum of inconvenience. Once, years ago, when I had a tiny house in Westminster, I gave shelter to a thin, battered alley cat whom I had found drenched with rain, crouched forlornly in the gardens outside the Houses of Parliament. For a little while, all was well, and life flowed by smoothly enough, with pussy

settling down, consuming large quantities of fish, and showing no desire to go out except for occasional sorties to the large variety of feline toilettes that were available in the surrounding backyards. Then one night, I was delayed in the country, and pussy was shut up all alone for twenty-four hours. I returned in some apprehension ... not because I was worried by any possible damage to carpets but because I hated to think that I had been the unwitting cause of embarrassment or even pain to a creature who had honoured me with its friendship.

I opened the door and called. No pussy. I walked into the little kitchen. The fish plate was wiped clean, even of the bones, the saucer of milk was empty ... but that could soon be remedied. I hurried up the stairs, still calling, and as I reached the top step I saw pussy emerging from the bathroom. I took her in my arms, and there was a soft purring, but I seemed to hear in the purring a faint echo of apprehension, as though she were not quite certain of her welcome. I sat her down; in a moment I would see to the fish and open the back window, but first I must wash my hands. I stepped into the bathroom, and as I did so, I saw that pussy had had the same idea; she too had washed her hands, with as much delicacy as was possible in the circumstances, precisely over the plug in the bath.

We do well to remember that cats are creatures of the jungle, that their eyes are lit with forest fires. But equally we should remember that they carry in their minds this strange understanding of some of the essentials of civilization, as though in some remote far-shadowed past they had dwelled in cities of their own building.

M stands for Mew.

Mews may be divided into three classes:

1. The sad mew
2. The conversational mew
3. The utilitarian mew.

There are several sub-divisions of these main categories. We will deal with them in due course.

1. Concerning the sad mew, we will not write, for these are meant to be happy pages, where we can, at least for a while, forget the sorrows of the world. All the fears and bewilderments of the little helpless creatures of the animal kingdom are reflected in the mew of a kitten that is lost. In real life we would not pass on, but here, we may.

2. The conversational mew is heard to its best advantage on a summer evening, when the cat is at the far end of the lawn and suddenly sees his master approaching. Whereupon the cat turns and begins to walk towards his master. As he walks, he talks. Needless to say, there are many pauses in this progress, for there are patches of grass to be sniffed, and fallen leaves to be inspected; but as soon as these duties are performed, the promenade is resumed ... always to the accompaniment of conversation. This is a sort of feline small talk; if it were translated it would probably be found to consist in comments on the weather, the extraordinary behaviour of the hedgehog under the copper beech, and the callousness of the gardener, whose weed-killer stings the paws. To which one would retort that it is better for pussy's paws to tingle for a few minutes than for pussy to be poisoned.

3. The utilitarian mew is most commonly heard outside closed doors. Even, I regret to say, outside some of the doors in my own house. For though there is a cat-door from the garden into my kitchen, and another cat-door from the kitchen into the dining-room, one cannot have cat-doors in every room.

Mews outside doors, it need hardly be said, should be instantly obeyed by cat-owners. How would the average human feel if every time he wished to leave the room he was obliged to sit on a mat and mew? However, lest it be assumed that we are carrying courtesy to extremes, we will admit that there are moments when, having opened a door for pussy, we have wished pussy would make up her mind as to whether she wants to go in or out. Only too often pussy remains poised half way, tail twitching, staring down the corridor, so that one cannot shut the door without endangering the tail. I have never been able to make up my mind whether it is permissible on such occasions to give pussy a slight prod. I admit that I have sometimes done this, but always at the cost of remorse.

Now for some of the variations on the three main classes of mew, which should be familiar to all serious students.

A. The purr-mew. This is one of the gentlest and most soothing sounds in a predominantly discordant world; it is the music made by a mother-cat to its kittens, particularly when her master leans over

the basket and strokes one of the kittens on its small, warm, square head. Then the purr-mew is heard at its best . . . a strange, treble trilling that breaks into a single note.

B. The almost silent mew. This is extremely subtle, and associated with moments of complete well-being and comfort. It is the faint sound that comes from a happy, sleepy cat, stretched out in front of a fire, when its master gently disturbs its dreams. One eyelid flickers, disclosing a line of liquid green, the mouth is very slightly opened, and then pianissimo comes this tiny sound, so faint that it is scarcely heard. After which the eyelid flickers back, the mouth is closed, and there is silence again. And the owner, if he has been properly brought up, tiptoes from the room.

C. The Siamese mew. This should perhaps be put in a class of its own, for it has a quite special timbre, and an exquisite resonance which must surely be the envy of all other felines. One has heard that there are some afflicted persons who are deaf to the beauty of the Siamese mew; such people, if they indeed exist, are deeply to be pitied. Should we ever encounter them we must be especially considerate to them, always remembering how much life has denied to them.[1] For the wild music of the Siamese mew is something without which no life can be considered quite complete. There is no true parallel to it, either in the world of nature or of art, and the only creatures who seem sometimes to echo this strange, bitter-sweet call are the gulls, wheeling inland when the wind is high.

[1] The mew is an infallible touchstone in exposing non-Fs who pose as Fs. Sometimes one is visited by people who, desiring to create a good impression, pretend to be fond of cats. When one's cat enters the room, these persons force a smile on their faces, and emit a hideous sound which is spelt MIAOW, thinking to ingratiate themselves (*a*) with the cat, and (*b*) with its master. Needless to say, the cat stares at them with horror and beats a hasty retreat. The owner, unfortunately, cannot follow its example. But at least he can be thankful that the non-F has revealed himself in his true colours, and if he has any sense he will take the first opportunity of locking up the silver.

N stands for Names.

The first of my cats of whom there is any historical record was a black kitten called Pasht. He appears on the third page of a novel called *Prelude*, which I wrote at the age of seventeen. I have just taken down a faded copy from my shelves to refresh my memory about him. Pasht plays a small but important role in the story. He was the last and most precious object to whom my hero, Paul—who was of course myself—said goodbye before leaving for his first day at the public school of Marlborough.

> Paul wandered slowly round the room saying goodbye to all the little things he loved. Suddenly he noticed a small black lump on the bed. It turned out to be Pasht, his kitten. It looked up at him with sleepy eyes, and put out a limp paw. Paul closed his eyes and rubbed his face in its short black fur. How cold its tiny nose was against his forehead! Oh God, how awful to have to say goodbye to this true faithful Pasht that he had loved for at least six weeks! He put him down and stared at the bed. Would he have a bed at Marlborough? He supposed they did have them there, but was by no means sure about it.

If I were in the habit of smiling wistfully, I should certainly do so after reading those lines. I may not have been a very nice boy—

there must surely be something wrong about seventeen-year-old novelists—but I seem to have had redeeming qualities.

The choice of Pasht as the name for a kitten suggests a certain schoolboy precocity, particularly when I remember that he was joined a year later by another black kitten whom I called Baudelaire. I had been caned, at school, for reading *Les Fleurs du Mal* in class. Admittedly, this may not be ideal literature for schoolboys, but there was so much fresh air at Marlborough, so many cold baths, so much hearty hymn-singing and so many small boys running about in shorts, obviously destined to be Low Church bishops, that a small dose of decadent and heavily perfumed French poetry might have been regarded as a healthy corrective. I suggested as much to my form master, who gave me ten strokes as a consequence. This treatment only enhanced my regard for the poet, and I sat down rather gingerly to learn by heart his sensuous poem 'Le Chat'. Some readers may recall its first, haunting lines:

> Viens, mon beau chat, sur mon cœur amoureux
> Retiens les griffes de ta patte,
> Et laise-moi plonger dans tes beaux yeux
> Mêlés de métal et d'agate.

Pasht and Baudelaire have long since passed on, though I hope that one day I may encounter them again. I cannot imagine a heaven without animals. (I find no sort of difficulty, on the other hand, in imagining a heaven without humans!) And whenever I conjure up a vision of the Pearly Gates, I find that black kittens always seem to find a place in it. They dart about making dabs at St Peter's robes, and very glossy and shiny their fur looks against the columns of the Gates, which, in my version, are made of extremely expensive mother-of-pearl.

But we were talking about names.

Have you noticed that other people's names for their cats are so often inapposite? For instance, one is introduced to an exceptionally refined creature with grey fur and topaz eyes, a cat who should spend a large part of its life gazing amiably on to a cathedral close, supervising the goings-on of the rural dean—and one is told that its name is Whiskey. How anybody can possibly attach the name of such a fluid to so delicious an object as a cat is beyond comprehension. Some cats, indeed, are given names which have a suspicion of actual contempt such as Smuts or Spotty. The true F, surely, should know better than this. Such names may be good for children, they are certainly not good enough for cats.

If history were properly taught at school—by which I mean that if cats and queens were treated with equal respect—there would be fewer examples of this unfortunate tendency. The pages of the past are richly studded with enchanting names given to their pets by illustrious Fs. One recalls the fourteen cats of Cardinal Richelieu, of which the prettiest—nominally—were Felimare, Soumise, Mimie Paillou and Perruque. Then there was Carlyle's Columbine—which needless to say was detested by Mrs Carlyle, who was as non-F as her husband was F. Dr Erasmus Darwin's cat was called Persian Snow, and Dickens's cat was called—not by him but by the family—Williamina. The mystic Evelyn Underhill had a St Philip Neri, Lytton Strachey owned a Tiberius, and Sir Walter Scott chose the name Hinse of Hinsefield.

All these names show a proper respect for felinity, which is all too rare even in the best F circles.

After these remarks the reader may well inquire why, for the last fifteen years or so, I have chosen to call my cats by numbers. There are three reasons.

Firstly, because I write a great deal of fiction, which demands the invention of a host of names to fit the personalities of the characters.

Few readers realize how irksome this invention is, how fatiguing. A name must fit a character like a glove, and unless it is the right name the creature refuses to play. Imagine how quite impossible the whole story of David Copperfield would have seemed if the hero had swopped names with Uriah Heep. This is an extreme case; the flamboyant labels which were permissible in the days of Dickens would not be acceptable today. But though a writer can no longer permit himself the extravagance of a Mr Veneering or a Pecksniff, Miss Codger or Betsey Prigg, he must still conjure up in his mind a name which fits in colour, in musical tone, in a hundred subtle associations.

(As a matter of minor literary interest, I always have recourse to the A.B.C. railway guide, at least as far as the surnames are concerned. Many English family names have a territorial origin, and the pages of this admirable volume are rich in unexpected treasures.)

The second reason why I call my cats by numbers is because in recent years numbers have acquired a subtle elegance of their own. Perhaps this is due to the influence of that remarkable woman Madame Chanel and her Numero Cinq. This agreeable essence was originally the perquisite of a few rich ladies of French society, but after the war, when Paris was occupied by the forces of the United States, it ended up by perfuming the entire American Army. In spite of this, the faint atmosphere of elegance still clings round the number, and when I was adopted by my first Siamese kitten I decided to call him Number One.

A word about these numbers. 'Two' and 'Three'—both Siamese—were tragedies. They died when they were still kittens, victims of that dire scourge of the feline world, the cat flu. I would like to think that all humans could put up so brave a fight for life as those two little kittens. After that, I swore that I would never have another Siamese—a vow that grows daily more difficult to keep.

Along came 'Four'. A kitten straight from the farm, black, perky, sentimental and altogether adorable. 'Four' has the best purr I have ever known, bar none, a purr with a quite astonishing vocal range. If he were not called 'Four' I should call him 'Callas', because his purr really has a prima donna quality. Moreover, it is still as sweet and flexible today as it was when he first jumped out of his basket. At the time of writing 'Four' is thirteen years old, which takes him, in human terms, well into the eighties. One wonders if the aforesaid diva will be purring quite so effectively at a similar age. One doubts it.

After 'Four' came 'Five', who is still very much with us, as you may have gathered.

'Six' presented us with a problem. He was an adorable shade of ginger, with spots on his nose, and paws as soft as a peach. But when

he strayed too far into the orchard ... which he often did ... and when we followed him, calling 'Six ... Six ... Six ...,' the result was, to say the least of it, inharmonious. If you will put down this volume for a moment, and say aloud the number six three times

in rapid succession, you will see what I mean. So we decided that 'Six' should be omitted . . . it should be The Cat Who Never Was, a mystic creature to tantalize our dreams. And 'Six' was rechristened 'Seven', and eventually—for this was a time of strife and turmoil—he was transported to the house of a very charming lady in Sussex, who had a kind heart and a large field and a number of old barns and outhouses in which he could prowl and hunt. Judging from the photographs which we sometimes receive of him, he has prowled and hunted to great effect.

Finally, came Oscar, who should have been 'Eight'. But he had already been christened, and as you may have gathered, he is a cat of such a vivid personality that any change of name would have been unthinkable.

Meanwhile, I lift a glass to 'Nine', 'Ten', 'Eleven' and 'Twelve', who are sleeping somewhere in the womb of Time. On the basis of the normal 'expectancy of life'—not only for myself but for my companions—'Twelve' should be the last. I shall welcome him when he comes, but as yet I have no desire to meet him face to face.

O stands for Old Maids.

And O also stands, as far as I am concerned, for a protest against the callousness and stupidity of the non-F world.

One of the commoner sneers against the cat is the suggestion that it is the favourite pet of old maids. Why this—even if it were true—should be regarded as a black mark against pussy, I am at a loss to understand. I have yet to learn that there is anything dishonourable either in old age or in solitude. And I consider it impertinence, indeed cruelty, to assume that because a woman has not married she has never had the chance to do so. There are countless reasons why a woman may not choose to marry, but if she is a true woman, she keeps them to herself. For which the world rewards her by sneering at her as an 'old maid'.

So if the cat does happen to be the favourite pet of the old maid, I think that this is a sign of excellent good sense of both parties. The life of an ageing, unmarried woman demands quiet friendship and gentle affection; it demands, above all, the companionship of a creature to whom home—the actual walls and windows and fireplaces and furnishings of home—are important and precious, apart from the human beings who inhabit them.

I often think that cats are 'house-proud'. Sometimes when I have paid a call at a house where a cat is in residence, I have felt a sharp eye fixed on me when I have been about to sit on a certain chair, as though pussy were saying: 'Kindly be careful with that chair; it's Hepplewhite and the legs are wonky.' And if the house happens to belong to one of the despised 'old maids' I feel that the cat is present in some subtle way in every part of the house and has, indeed, taken part in its arrangement. I can guess her favourite corners, can see how she would stretch out on the hearthrug, so close to the fire that you would think the fur of her tummy would be scorched, can picture her staring out of the window, and can even hear her, in imagination, making those extremely unrefined chattering noises at the birds.

An old house, old furniture, old pictures and ornaments, the faint scent of lavender in a bowl, and an old maid sitting by the fire with a cat on her lap . . . what a perfect picture for the ridicule of the world! How deliciously amusing! Let's chuck a stone through her window!

But the old maid legend, of course, has no justification in fact. One does not usually associate the personnel of the British Navy with old maidishness, particularly the members of the lower deck, but sailors, ever since the Navy sailed the seas, have demanded that cats should come too, and have lavished on them quite remarkable affection even to the extent of risking their lives for them. The non-F may suggest that this is merely because the cat is a rat-catcher. To which the F has a ready retort. If the engineers who design such a streamlined monster as the modern aircraft carrier are unable to prevent their ships from being overrun by rats without invoking the superior technical abilities of pussy, they should hang their heads in shame.

This reminds me of a story narrated to me by the very gallant captain of a very glorious ship—the *Ark Royal*, which led the Germans such a thrilling dance in the early days of the war. The *Ark Royal* had its own feline contingent, consisting of a motley but exuberant collection of pussies collected by affectionate sailors, usually in somewhat alcoholic moments, from such places as Plymouth and Pompey. Whenever the ship came to a foreign port these pussies, it seems, were as anxious to go ashore as the sailors themselves; indeed, they insisted on their rights, and lined up with their tails erect and their whiskers bristling, as soon as the gangways were lowered. After all, if sailors could have a wife in every port, so could pussies. And husbands, too, it appeared, judging from several accouchements which took place after a courtesy visit to Naples.

But I was supposed to be telling a story. Here it is. Every time those pussies went ashore the captain of this great ship, who was of course impeccably F, heaved a sigh of regret and said to himself: 'Well, I suppose that we have said goodbye to them. I hope they fare well, but we shall never see them again.' A very reasonable assumption, as you will agree. For how could the pussies know when the ship was setting sail again? How could they guess that their leave

expired in precisely forty-eight hours, and that if they were late they would be left behind?

And yet, they always *did* know. Some strange feline jungle telegraph sent its mysterious messages through the back streets and alleys of Naples or Malta or Mauritius, or wherever the ship might be, and out came the pussies shortly before sailing time, padding silently along towards the docks, greeting one another—one likes to think—with stories of adventure and romance. Sometimes they cut things very fine, so that the last gangway would be on the point of being raised when the last pussy rushed aboard. But they always knew, so the admiral swore, and I was brought up to believe that admirals never tell a lie.

The affection of sailors should be enough to dispel the legend that the cat is only the old maids' darling, but history abounds in examples of many other brave men whose hearts have warmed to a purr and melted to a mew. Abraham Lincoln is not normally regarded as a missish type, and yet, during one of the most anxious moments of the Civil War, he had time to spare to save three deserted kittens from starvation. The episode occurred in General Grant's camp. Lincoln stumbled upon them in a deserted tent. The campaign was in a crucial stage, his heart must have been burdened with crushing cares, but Lincoln lifted up the kittens and smuggled them under his coat and did not leave them till he had seen that they would be properly cared for.

But why quote further examples of pussy's eminent friends? After all, we decided that O should stand for Old Maids. And even if cats had been created solely for them, their role would be important enough. To bring solace to the lonely and gaiety to the ageing, to give to each separate day a constant variety and to life, as a whole, a soft purring rhythm ... could we, with reason, ask for more?

P stands for Purring.

Purring, in humans, is a rare accomplishment. Often a novelist will make one of his characters speak in a 'soft, purring voice', but the metaphor is inept; there may be a faint illusion of purring but it remains an illusion. Why? Because though the vast majority of humans can purr out, they cannot purr in. This is due to the inferior flexibility of the human tongue muscles. Try it for yourself. Take a deep breath and exhale, allowing the tongue to vibrate against the palate. You will achieve quite a passable imitation of a purr. Now try to do the same thing backwards, inhaling. You will achieve nothing but a distasteful sucking noise.

I once met a man with an almost perfect purr, in as well as out. He was an admiral of the fleet, and he was staying with the Governor of Gibraltar, with whom I was dining. How we began to talk about purring I cannot recollect, but you may imagine my delight when I discovered that so distinguished a man was gifted with so exceptional a talent. There he sat, in the candlelight, fingering the stem of his wine-glass, purring with supreme virtuosity. His uniform was ablaze with decorations, and I remember thinking how ironic it was that none of them had been awarded for purring.

When I was planning this little volume I wrote to the admiral asking if I might mention him by name. He replied, politely but firmly, that he would prefer to remain anonymous. He seemed to imagine that his gift, if widely known, might lead to adverse comment on the lower deck. I cannot believe that this was his true reason; I suspect that he really feared that it might make the other admirals jealous.

Hassan, my Indian bearer during the latter part of the war, was another man with an authentic two-way purr. This was by no means his only claim to originality; he had, for example, a remarkable flair for dress. Soon after I had engaged him, I was bidden to stay with the Viceroy at Delhi, and I told Hassan that he must smarten himself up if he wished to accompany me. The Viceroy's servants, I remembered, were very grand in scarlet and gold, and Hassan looked like a sort of pirate. So I gave him money to get a new outfit. For two days he disappeared, and I was about to give him up as a bad job, and engage another man, when suddenly he came back, looking more like a pirate than ever. His method of getting a new outfit had been to search the bazaars and the junk-shops for a mass of military decorations, badges, ribbons, cap-bands, stripes and symbols of every description, which he had proudly sewn on to his jacket. I pretended to be annoyed, though I was in fact enchanted, and to put me in a good humour—for he knew I loved cats—he suddenly lowered his head and began to purr, a deep, rich purr in and out, of impeccable felinity. He was a great success with the Viceroy, who informed me that nothing quite like him had ever entered the portals of Vice-regal Lodge before, which I can well believe.

Hassan eventually purred himself out of my life in Madras, accompanied by my cuff links, my cigarette case and a large wad of rupees which he had abstracted from my wallet in a fit of absent-mindedness. It was an expensive purr, but it was worth it.

The most exquisite purr I have known, a real prima donna of a purr, belongs to my own cat 'Four'. It has all the qualities which connoisseurs of purring esteem most highly ... a perfect *vibrato*, superb breath control, exquisite quality of tone and a quite exceptional range, which stretches from a rich contralto to a flawless E in alt. There is no role where purring is demanded which 'Four' could not play with the greatest distinction. Moreover, 'Four' needs no human encouragement to make him perform; like all great artists he purrs for the sake of purring. Often, when I have been sitting at my desk, without knowing that he was near me, I have been suddenly startled by the fluting sounds of 'Four's' purr, and I look down to see him gazing at me ... rather in the manner of a prima donna who is waiting for her accompanist.

'Five' has a gentle, pleasing purr, but he would be the last to describe himself as a great artist; he excels in other spheres. Oscar has talent and energy but his purr is undisciplined and his enthusiasm runs away with him. As we noted in a previous chapter, he is inclined, out of sheer emotion, to dribble. This usually occurs when I am having breakfast in bed, and I have discovered a simple way of stopping it. (The student who has read D for Dilapidations will recall that Oscar had a regrettably Bohemian upbringing.) To interrupt him in the middle of an aria would be unkind and humiliating, so I usually allow him to have his purr out, and in the meantime I tactfully slide a copy of the *Financial Times* under him, to deal with the dribbles. The perusal of this journal, throughout my life, has been so uniformly depressing that I am glad to be able to put it to some practical use.

All Fs will have their own pet varieties of the exquisite art of purring. Some prefer their purrs pianissimo ... the sort of faint, sweet song that comes from a kettle that one leaves on the hob, by a log fire. Some demand greater volume, and will go to any lengths of stroking and cosseting to produce loud and brilliant purrs which will arouse envy in the hearts of other Fs, whose pussies are not so accomplished. But nearly all will agree that the best purr of all, the purr that speaks most directly to the heart, is the first faint purr that comes from a frightened stray, that one has found in the rain and taken in one's arms and coaxed with confidence. This is the purr that is quite irresistible, the language that only a brute would fail to heed.

Q stands for Query.

The mind of the cat is a jungle abounding in marks of interrogation, through which Fs can find their way by instinct, while non-Fs flounder and are lost and frightened. Why should this be? Why is the world divided—as it evidently is—into two classes, F and non-F? Here is a suitable moment for examining this fascinating problem.

Let me state at the outset that I do not regard the non-F's dislike of cats as an affectation. If a man shrinks back in horror as soon as 'Five' walks into the room, and stares at him as though he were some dreadful apparition from Outer Space, I am prepared to concede that he is really expressing a genuine emotion, and not putting on an act. All I would observe, in passing, is that some non-Fs seem to be rather proud of their non-Fness, as though it were in some way associated with the heroic virtues. But is it? When females are being rescued from burning buildings is the doggy man always the first up the ladder, while the cat-lover slinks away, in craven shame, into the shadows? No doubt some would say so. But I would like some rather more definite proof.

The popular novelists are largely responsible for this artificial division of human and animal nature, in which all the broad-shouldered, blue-eyed V.C.s are put in one pen, smoking pipes and surrounded by adoring cocker spaniels, while all the decadents are put in another, inhaling Turkish cigarettes and muttering sinister things to Siamese kittens. In spite of Freud, much of the psychology of the modern best-seller is still so shallow that when a novelist wishes to darken the character of one of his puppets all he has to do is to cause a dog to snarl at him, the assumption being that the dog has a sort of psychic nose for evil. This is really rather unfair; if it were true a great many of us would be revealed in a most unbecoming light—including myself. For many years my visits to the house of a devoted friend were complicated, to put it mildly, by the presence of two gigantic Alsatians who obviously regarded me with the utmost disfavour. They were the size of Shetland ponies, they had gleaming yellow fangs, and their barks, echoing through the long gallery of the entrance hall, were so deafening and so prolonged that for the first ten minutes after arriving one had to shout to make oneself heard. They never actually bit me but one day, to my great satisfaction, they bit a fellow guest, twice, on the behind. And he *had* broad shoulders, and he *had* blue eyes, and he *was* a V.C. Which 'only goes to show', as my old nanny used to observe.

But no novelist would ever permit his hero, and a V.C. at that, to be bitten on the behind by an Alsatian, or even by a rather petulant Borzoi. Scratched by a cat—yes, *that* would accord with all the manly virtues, and might even be interpreted as a token of virility; bitten by a dog—no, it would be totally out of character, like being kicked by a horse. And now that we are on this subject, let us consider this question of horses. (In modern Britain, one is indeed compelled to consider them. The shadow of the horse looms so large over British society that one wonders why the *Court Circular* is not renamed the *Equine Gazette*.)

As I have distinct partiality for almost anything on four legs, I can claim a quite genuine affection for horses, provided that they are old and solid, with shaggy manes, in a pleasing shade of Rembrandt brown, and leaning over rustic gates. Otherwise, I must confess, I can dispense with horses. Quite frankly, they alarm me. I think that the noise they make through their nostrils, on occasions, is positively macabre, and I do not care whether it is *joie de vivre*, rage, or simply acute sinus; it terrifies me. Also, they kick, hard. And they look as though they bite, and I suspect that they do, though I have never really explored this question. On the very few occasions when I have stayed at grand houses where people have stables, and when we have gone off to 'see the horses' before luncheon, I have usually managed to slink off and strike up an acquaintance with the stable cat.

All this has taken us a long way from our original question. *Why* is mankind divided into two classes, F and non-F? Maybe there is no final answer to this question. And yet, some years ago, in a French scientific journal whose name I have forgotten—(I picked it up in the waiting-room of a doctor in the rue de Lille)—I read a theory that seemed to make sense. Apparently some doctor in Toulouse had made an experiment with several hundred babies of all descriptions, male, female, white, brown and black, ranging in age from three to eighteen months. These creatures were disposed in perambulators, and various French pussies were introduced to them. Nine per cent of the infants, even before they had seen the pussies, went into brisk convulsions providing that pussy was to the windward of them; if pussy was on the other side there was no reaction. The obvious assumption was that non-Fness is in some manner connected with the sense of smell—an assumption that would vindicate the claim made by some Fs that they are aware of the presence of a cat in a room even if it is for the moment invisible.

To Fs, this will seem a curious excuse for non-Fness. Compared with most animals, the cat is singularly inoffensive. Indeed, I have a distinct partiality for the odour of fur, particularly after pussy has been performing her ablutions; it has the same faint fragrance that comes from damp moss, which is a great deal more than one can say for most human beings.

So perhaps we had better leave the question unanswered. There are Fs and non-Fs; we will leave it at that. But I do not see that we need necessarily assume that never the twain shall meet. All we would suggest is that at least we meet on a level of equality.

R stands for *rubato* or *rallentando* . . .

though any other musical expression would serve as well. For here we shall discuss cats and music, beginning with the first introduction of the new kitten to the wonders of the grand pianoforte.

Looking back on my life, a large part of it seems to have been spent on my knees, coaxing kittens from under sofas in music-rooms, after they have been unnecessarily alarmed by my rendering of Chopin's second Scherzo. If this were indeed the case, my life would have been well conducted, for there could surely be no pleasanter combination of circumstances than Chopin, a music-room, and a new kitten. However, my memory is probably exaggerating; memory often does, when it is summoning up the ghosts of past delights. How many golden hours one seems to be able to recall, lying on the burning sands of the Mediterranean! When one adds them up they really amount to a few weeks in Cannes, which were usually marked by a series of cloudbursts.

To return to the kitten and the piano, it is vitally important, at the beginning of the operation, that the kitten should be in a mood of complete relaxation. All nervous tensions must have been eased. Ping-pong balls must have been replaced in drawers, pieces of screwed-up paper must have been removed from sight. The kitten's tummy, if possible, should be full. The mood should be one of luxury and repletion, and it should be enhanced by a judicious application of the various arts of stroking, which are fully enunciated under the letter S.

These physical conditions having been ensured, the kitten may be lifted up, like a ball in the palm of the hand, and gently placed on a bound copy of the Sonatas of Mozart, which is lying on top of the piano. Here, we are perhaps being unduly perfectionist. No great crisis will ensue if one places the kitten on an unbound copy of the Sonatas of Beethoven—or, for that matter, on any solid volume of classical music. What would happen if one were to place it on a volume of jazz I do not know, for the simple reason that such an object has not, so far, been admitted to my house.

One may now take one's seat at the piano, put one's foot on the soft pedal, and very gently strike the note G in alt. Here again we may be accused of undue perfectionism; G flat would do as well, or G sharp; the point to be observed is that the note should be reasonably high and extremely soft. A loud note in the bass would immediately suggest growls, and the kitten's musical education might suffer a serious setback.

The effect of this first note will vary according to the kitten's temperament. On some it may be nearly disastrous—there may be a wild leap from the piano on to the floor, and a frenzied escape into the garden, if one has been so unwise as to leave the door open. In such cases, there will be a long and difficult road ahead, in which one continues to strike G in alt, day after day, until the kitten is at last convinced that one is not invoking the voice of the devil.

Such cases, fortunately, are few and far between. More often the reaction is roughly as follows:

First G.	Saucer eyes, swift glances to the right and left, and a step backward.
Second G.	Wider saucer eyes, more glances, and a step forward.
Third G.	Widest of all saucer eyes, crouching, and several steps forward to the edge of the piano.

When this stage is reached, the F may use his own discretion. There will, of course, be more strokings, and more soothing and melodious words. In my own experience I have found it helpful, before striking G for the fourth time, to tap the wire of the note with my fingernail; and then, if this arouses interest, to draw the nail gently across several wires—an action which produces a pleasing and faintly plaintive sound which is not unfeline in quality.

The vital point, as always, is to try to enter into pussy's mind and to shrink oneself to pussy's proportions, so that one can imagine how it feels to be hoisted on to a black shiny mountain and transported to the edge of a dark cavern, from whose interior strange wails and howls are echoing. Most humans, in such circumstances, would probably go nearly mad, and spend the rest of their lives being psychoanalysed.

We now enter the realm of traveller's tales. I would not care to make a definite assertion that cats are musical, but I have a strong suspicion that they are not unmusical, by which I mean that ugly sounds distress them. My own cats, quite definitely, dislike the various forms of cacophony which, in these days, are lumped under the generic name of 'jazz'. Even in the best regulated households, these sounds sometimes intrude, in spite of all the precautions that may be taken against them. Young people come to dine, bearing with them these shining, sinister discs of discord; they drift over to the gramophone and put them on and jig about the room to the resultant uproar. One likes young people, one tries to be a good host, and one has the faint hope that one may not yet be quite old enough to be cast for the role of Scrooge. So one allows the uproar to continue.

But it is with some satisfaction that one notes that 'Four' has risen from the chair in which he was comfortably asleep, and is stalking from the room with some hauteur, casting a look of unmitigated disgust at the instrument from which the horrible sounds are pouring.

'Four' has never left the room when I am playing Chopin and sometimes I dare to think that one green eye opens, and regards me with approval, when the slow movement of the Grieg Concerto is going rather better than usual. However that may be, cats and music have always been linked in my mind, and always will be. The basket of kittens in the nursery—and the exercises by Stephen Heller; the incredibly old Blüthner in the drawing-room of my boyhood, and the incredibly old black cat who used to sit on top of it; pianos galore, cats galore. Even in the concert hall . . . even, I dare to say it, during the music of Mozart . . . ghostly felines have a way of drifting across the stage, for Mozart, as we have previously observed, was F from tip to toe. (I nearly wrote from tip to tail.) And so was Chopin and so was Brahms, and so were Delius and Tschaikowski and César Franck and . . . But I seem to be drifting back to my foreword. The one thing we must never forget is that Wagner was non-F. He was a great black dog, growling in the bass and howling to the moon.

S stands for Stroking.

Stroking is a delicate art, whose subtleties are little understood by non-Fs. Even some Fs have much to learn about it. In any properly organized society there would be State schools to teach the elements of deportment towards felines. In such schools, stroking would be one of the most important of all the students' courses.

Several volumes might—and certainly should—be written about the charming occupation of cat-stroking. After all, this is a perfect example of an occasion when the human and animal kingdoms are united in complete harmony, a harmony which is expressed by the music of the purr. However, as space is restricted, we must be content with a few generalizations.

Surprising as it may seem, there is only one form of stroking which is acceptable at *all* times in *all* circumstances by *all* felines. This is . . .

(A) *The Under-the-Chin Stroke*. The importance of this form of stroking may be very simply tested. Supposing that the student is walking down a street, and is lucky enough to encounter a cat sitting on a wall. He will naturally desire to strike up an acquaintance even—or in some cases especially—if the cat is battered and tough, with, in all probability, a touch of cynicism. If he walks straight up and tries to stroke it on the back, he may quite rightly receive a scratch for his pains. After all, he is a stranger and his motives may be suspect; he has not yet established a stroking relationship nor created a stroking atmosphere.

How then must the student conduct himself? Very slowly and gently, so that pussy may follow his every movement, he must advance his hand, with the wrist in an advanced position. Here he must pause to study pussy's reactions. If they are favourable he may advance his hand further, with the wrist still forward, and only when the wrist is almost touching pussy's chin should he extend the fingers and begin the stroking movement.

As soon as contact has been established, the stroking may proceed with increasing energy. Accomplished Fs will not need to be told that this is a moment when many pleasing variations may be introduced. Of these perhaps the most technically difficult is the clenched fist stroke, which explains itself—the fist is tightly clenched and the knuckles are rubbed briskly, indeed almost violently, on the side of the chin. Some cats, whose experience of professional stroking is unfortunately limited, may at first express surprise at this development, but it will only be a matter of a few seconds before they begin to co-operate.

(B) *The Back Stroke*. This is, of course, the conventional form of stroking, familiar to F and non-F alike—and alas, in the hands of the latter, what a very bourgeois and uninspiring exercise it usually proves to be! A few casual dabs at pussy's back and a feeble twiddly scratching of pussy's head. No subtlety of finger work, no attempt at *vibrato*, no sense of rhythm. To watch a non-F engaged in back-stroking is to be reminded of the essential crudity of the human race.

Fs will agree that the apparent simplicity of back-stroking is highly deceptive. It is like the music of Mozart which looks so easy that you would think a child could play it, whereas, in fact, it demands an impeccable technique. Indeed, the task of the back-stroker is even more difficult than the task of the musician. Once one has mastered, let us say, the Adagio of the eighteenth sonata in D major one can play it on any piano, provided that the instrument is in tune; all keyboards are identical. But no cats are identical; their backs vary in size, shape, texture and resilience; with each new cat one must begin, in every sense of the phrase, from scratch.

Only a few elemental examples can here be offered as a guide to those non-Fs who, let us hope, have learned the error of their ways and wish to join the ranks of civilized—i.e. advanced back-stroking—society. Since we have used the musical metaphor, we will continue it. To begin with, we would suggest . . .

1. *The Andante Stroke*. This is a slow, simple movement in which the principal agent is the palm of the hand. The stroke should begin at the base of the neck and stop approximately two inches before the tail. The phrasing should be, of course, legato, and the tempo should be a strict 2/4 to the bar.

This stroke may be used, with mutual pleasure and profit, on tranquil occasions when pussy is sitting in front of a log fire, when the room is filled with the fragrance of apple wood, and when the golden shadows on the ceiling are like the blossoms of ghostly laburnums, swaying in the wind.

2. *Staccato con brio*. This is a highly effective stroke, which may at first appear to the non-F as beyond his technical capacity. However, in spite of its superficial brilliance, it is not as difficult as might be imagined. One could compare it, in this respect, to that old concert chestnut 'The Rustle of Spring', whose facile arpeggios have dazzled generations of simple audiences in village halls.

The *staccato con brio* stroke should be reserved for festive occasions, when the mood is gay and dancing, and is perhaps best practised in the open air. Both hands are used, in order to execute a series of swift staccato scales, beginning on the crown of the head and ending with a brilliant passage down the tail. Lightness of touch is absolutely essential. If the student does not feel quite happy about his rendering of this stroke, he would be well advised to spend a few weeks at the pianoforte, perfecting some of the more elaborate cadenzas of Liszt.

(C) *Tummy-Rubbing*. There appear to be three schools of feline thought about tummy-rubbing.

Members of the first school are quite evidently bored by the whole procedure. Although they may assume a tummy-rubbing posture, and dispose themselves on the hearth-rug with both paws languidly crossed over their chests, as soon as the tummy-rubbing begins their faces register intense ennui, and they regard the tummy-rubber with cold contemptuous eyes, as if demanding that he should immediately cease this nonsense, and turn his fingers to some more profitable exercise.

Members of the second school of thought are actively hostile. At the first suggestion of tummy-rubbing they will 'back-pedal' violently, as a signal that they are not amused.

Members of the third school, however—approximately seventy per cent of the feline world—find a certain amount of intelligent tummy-rubbing essential to their peace of mind. The accent is on the word intelligent. Tummy-rubbing is not to be performed as though one were brushing a hearth-rug. Only the tips of the fingers should be used. As a rough guide the tempo is 4/4 and the mood is *andante moderato*. (In the case of Siamese, omit the *moderato*.) The movement should be spiral, and from time to time, if the tummy-rubbing is proceeding smoothly, the tail may be very delicately pulled.

A Note on Stroking Neuters

The sensation of being stroked on the back, in the case of some neuters, is so exceedingly agreeable that it causes them to assume postures which might possibly be regarded as inelegant. My own cat 'Four', for example, if firmly stroked, crouches on his front legs and elevates his behind so sharply that his whole body is hoisted at an angle of forty-five degrees. Moreover, having adopted this attitude, he is apt to remain in it for several minutes, even after the stroking has stopped. On occasions this habit has caused embarrassment to visitors. They enter a room, they observe a feline apparently transfixed in what seems to them a singular attitude, and they jump to extraordinary conclusions.

I cannot offer the student any absolutely infallible advice in this dilemma, apart from the suggestion that he should announce that he is not at home to visitors. However, if the posture strikes him as exaggerated, he may slightly modify it by combining back-stroking with chin-stroking; this will normally cause pussy's posterior to sink by about five degrees. He may also, in extreme cases, give pussy a gentle push on to the carpet. In this position there are various other technical devices by which he may gradually soften pussy's ardour, such as nose-rubbing and a very gentle variation of the aforementioned *staccato con brio*.

I must apologize if the foregoing paragraphs give a slightly non-F impression. I need hardly say that the true F will find nothing unnatural or embarrassing in the sight of a cat whose behind is hoisted at such a precipitous angle. However, I am aware that non-Fs are basically anthropomorphic, and are apt to translate pussy's reactions into human terms, so that they unconsciously see themselves, or their female friends, sitting on the carpet in a similar position. I should be the first to agree that this would be, indeed, a most distasteful spectacle.

T stands for Trivia.

It might have stood for Toms or Tails or Tabbies. Indeed, I was actually pondering which of these important subjects to discuss, when something happened. A single crimson petal from a bowl of peonies dropped lazily on to the rug in front of the fire-place. At the same time 'Four' darted out from under the sofa, and flicked the petal with his paw, so that it was tossed up into a shaft of sunlight. And I realized that this was one of those flashes of happiness that I shall recall for the rest of my life. Not because there was anything strange or spectacular about it, but because cats have an extraordinary capacity for making single moments seem dramatic, so that they linger for ever in one's memory. I feel that a cat must have been in the room when Rupert Brooke wrote:

One instant I, an instant, knew,
As God knows all. And it and you
I, above Time, oh, blind! could see
In witless immortality.
I saw the marble cup; the tea,
Hung on the air, an amber stream;
I saw the fire's unglittering gleam,
The painted flame, the frozen smoke...

So it was on this occasion. I shall remember the peony petal and the way it glowed, for a brief second, as it caught the sun. I shall remember putting down my pen, and staring at the petal, and listening to the song of a thrush singing in the dark branches of the copper beech. I shall remember, too, how my mind set off, not for the first time, on the least fruitful of all philosophical explorations, examining the pros and cons of predestination. If the Universe is not to be regarded as a senseless chaos, if there is indeed a master plan, in which no detail is left to chance, then from the beginning of time it must have been ordained that my peony petal should fall at precisely that moment. Moons have waxed and waned, winds have driven across the earth, waters have ebbed and swollen, seeds and roots have struggled for survival, through countless centuries, simply in order to achieve the desired result of a single petal falling, a black cat leaping, and a shaft of sunlight catching a patch of crimson.

If this is not the case, if the petal fell by blind chance, then anything can fall by chance, including those comforting sparrows. Houses can fall by chance, and bombs and meteors ... and oh dear me this is all getting too depressing. It is the fault of 'Four', who is something of a philosopher himself, and firmly on the side of predestination when it is a matter of fish.

I wonder if there are any other people, with reasonable claims to sanity whose minds attach little feline tags to all sorts of unsuitable objects. Consider the question of furniture. I happen to be fond of paying my half-crown and prowling round old houses where there are fine examples of eighteenth-century walnut, and constantly when I have been examining a Chippendale chair or a Hepplewhite bureau I have been startled by seeing, or seeming to see, a ghostly paw protruding between the legs. This is because there stands by the side of my desk a charming Chippendale waste-paper basket, in a sort of open Chinese latticework, through which Oscar frequently puts his paw in order to dab at the crumpled pieces of paper inside. On one occasion Oscar developed such a passionate interest in the waste-paper basket, sniffing it, and poking his paws in it and standing on his hind legs against it, that for an awful moment I feared that it might be sheltering some unfortunate refugee in the shape of a mouse. Investigation proved it to be not a mouse but an olive stone, which somebody had dropped into the basket after a cocktail party. Oscar has a morbid craving for olives, and before any party they have to be kept firmly locked up in the pantry.

There's another fascinating topic for all trivia ... cats and food. In any place where cat-lovers are gathered together, sooner or later the subject of food will be eagerly discussed, with particular emphasis on any pussy who has peculiar tastes. (My own contribution, on these occasions, is the story of one of my earliest cats, who was called Beresford. He had a passion for the pulpy inside of melons.) Often there is a strong streak of masochism in these stories. 'My dear,' exclaims an excited lady, '*can* you guess what that wicked Tibby did last night? John had somebody *terribly* important to dinner and I bought a jar of caviare from Fortnum's—not the red sort but the *enormous* grey sort—and Tibby gobbled the lot just before dinner!' This story causes her confidante to shudder with delight and embark on some story to prove that her own pussy is capable of equally outrageous behaviour. Let us be honest, most of us rather like our cats to have a streak of wickedness. I should not feel quite easy in the company of any cat that walked about the house with a saintly expression, never scratching the chairs.

That word 'scratching' sets one's mind off again, into the lumber-room of memory ... and what a host of trivia it discovers! But are they all trivia? I wonder. Let me tell you a story. In my last winter at Merry Hall, a house which I greatly loved, I had to cut down an old pear tree. This is a horrible thing to have to do, at any time; it is a form of murder; but in this case it was particularly distasteful because it happened to be a tree which had been a favourite of my Siamese cat 'One', who had often climbed up in its branches. So when the tree was being cut down I went away for the week-end, which may strike some people as showing an excess of sensibility. I do not greatly care.

Came the spring—a cold, acid spring which made great demands on the central heating. I said to Gaskin: 'We'd better start on the logs from that old pear tree; they should burn by now.' So the logs were brought into the music-room, and I laid a fire of bits and pieces and set the first branch of pear wood on the top.

Then, as the flames began to flicker round it, I noticed something strange about the bark. It was flecked and scarred with a thousand tiny marks. Suddenly, I realized the significance of those marks. They were the signs of 'One's' scratching. I had never known that this was his special scratching tree, for its bark had always been hidden by a thick growth of shrubs, but so it must have been. Year in and year out he must have wandered out on his mysterious errands, and pushed his way through the jungle of the shrubbery, stretched out his paws and tautened his back and indulged in this strange rite of scratching. And in the end, 'One' had sickened and lost his hold on life . . . this was two years before . . . and I had been compelled to arrange for him to be put away.

Two deaths—the death of a faithful friend and the death of a tree. And for both of them I had been responsible. The flames flickered and curled round the log, slowly the scratch marks were darkened, and then there was only flame and smoke, drifting up the chimney. There was a terrible finality about that moment, as though a chapter in my life were closing, indeed, a whole series of chapters.

T for Trivia? Again, I wonder. For if a scratch on a tree can make one feel that the whole world is in mourning, what happens when one is confronted by the real tragedies of life?

U stands for Under the Walnut Tree.

This title, I confess, is sheer cheating. But what is one to do? I wanted to write about battle and conflict among cats—all the strange pomps and circumstances of feline War, all the mysterious physical and psychic influences that suddenly cause their backs to arch, their legs to stiffen, and their bodies to be switched into that extraordinary and very frightening position in which pussy is broadside on, with a fierce and bristling tail at the alert.

But there were no letters left to fit these grim occasions. B, which might have stood for Battle, had already been annexed for the comparatively gentle art of Beeing, as you may remember. As for the letter W, which might have stood for War . . . that had already been reserved for a thesis on Weaving.

And yet, there is some slight justification for this technical trick. For in my new garden—which is in fact a very old garden and, I hope, my last—there is an immense walnut tree, whose branches have been moulded by time into a design of muscular beauty. In the shade of this walnut tree the first conflicts have been waged between 'Four', 'Five' and Oscar on the one hand, and Rudolph and Pemberton on the other. (They are the cats next door.) In this same shade, sentry watch is undertaken, and major decisions of strategy decided.

When I first encountered Rudolph and Pemberton, I had a dim hope that they might make friends with my own family. They were both of the greatest amiability, very sleek and plump, one ginger and one tabby. Before we moved in, they had an engaging habit of walking up the little path of the cottage, and strolling in through the front door, as though the place belonged to them. In the lifetime of the previous owner, apparently, they had been made welcome, and given fish—not that they really needed it—and encouraged to leap on beds. I thought how pleasant it would be to continue this admirable tradition.

I was a fool, of course. On the very first night that 'Four', 'Five' and Oscar were given their latchkeys—by which I mean the first night on which we felt it would be safe to open the cat-doors—I was woken in the small hours by the familiar cacophony, rising and falling, ebbing and swelling, drifting through the open window. Not that I find the sound of caterwauling, in itself, distasteful; indeed, compared with the noise emitted by the average television crooner it is as sweet as the breath of lutes and the sigh of harps, echoing down some Elysian valley. All that worries me when I hear caterwauling is the knowledge that the woodwind motif, as it were, may suddenly give way to a passage of percussion, and lead to scratched noses and bitten ears.

Which was precisely what happened at this moment. The woodwind rose to incredible heights in minor thirds, gained steadily in volume, and suddenly broke, literally, into percussion as a flowerpot was knocked off a window ledge to the accompaniment of a fusillade of hisses, punctuated by a few *ad lib.* cadenzas in alt. I sprang to the window, and shouted and clapped my hands, and made all the usual futile noises. Dark shapes flitted away from under the chequered shadows of the walnut tree and once again there was silence.

But war had been declared, and I fear that it continues to this day.

Why do cats fight?

Why do two beautiful bundles of fur, who might wander off together, exchanging sniffs and purrs and confidences, immediately transform themselves into a pair of crook-backed, howling demons of destruction?

Once again, I think that this is a problem which might be firmly deposited, like the problem of the cat and the mouse, on the lap of the Almighty. And having done so, we might turn to address a few words to the non-F, who is inclined to reach for the nearest brick at the least sign of feline conflict.

'At least' . . . so we should address the non-F . . . 'the battles of cats are far less deplorable, far less morally reprehensible, than the battles of men.'

When cats fight they fight as individuals, driven by the storms and stresses of Nature, in whose soul there is always conflict. They do not march in serried lines, like an exceptionally stupid breed of sheep, to the command of a cackle from a radio.

Legions of tabbies do not suddenly advance across Richmond Bridge in order to destroy legions of Siamese, lined up on the opposite bank, merely because some pampered Persian . . . whom none of them has ever met . . . has ordered them to do so. Well, they don't, do they? Yet this is precisely what men do.

Battalions of black cats from the East End do not suddenly lose their reason, and band together, and charge up Park Lane in order to battle to the death with opposing battalions of white cats from the West End, merely because some cat in the suburbs . . . who was probably a dingy shade of brown, anyway . . . has thought up some idiotic slogan about the supremacy of white (or black) races. Yet that is precisely what men do.

From all of this we may conclude that pussy, waging her intensely personal conflicts in the shadow of the walnut tree, presents a somewhat less ugly picture than Man, waging his coldly impersonal conflicts on whatever battlefield may be the vogue at the moment. All the same, I regret these feline conflicts. Even when hostilities are not actually in progress, they are in the air. And always they centre round the walnut, for the branches of this ancient tree spread far across the outbuildings, casting their shade over the roof of the old tool-shed, and this roof has been chosen by 'Four', 'Five' and Oscar as a sort of outpost, from which they may repel any sorties from Rudolph and Pemberton.

Even as I write, they are sitting there like sentries, silent, immobile except for an occasional lashing of the tail, eternally at the alert. And there, on the opposite wall, sit Rudolph and Pemberton, also silent, also immobile . . . except for the aforesaid tail lashing. And I walk up the little staircase and look out of the crooked window and heave a sigh and think how idiotic it all is. They might be playing together, they might be sniffing and dabbing and chasing each other. But no, they do no such thing. They only sit and glare. One would think they had all been reading the morning's edition of the *Daily Worker*.

V stands for Verses.

Inevitably, pussy has inspired a great deal of poetry throughout the ages, and inevitably most of it is very bad indeed. (Though not nearly as bad as the poems which have been inspired by dogs.) Oddly enough, most of the really atrocious feline verse has been written by men . . . strong and usually silent men, too. Large, muscular Christians, living impeccable lives in cathedral closes, have gazed into pussy's eyes, gasped with delight, and burst into verses of incredible archness. They have gurgled about pussy's toes and tinkled about her tail and shuddered with ecstasy as she weaves around their gaiters. The women have been comparatively restrained and have managed to keep their humour, like the American lady who wrote

O lovely bit
Of silky fur
Jewel-eyed
Aristocrat
I'd wear you
To the Opera
If you were
Not my cat.

From time to time, however, a great poet has looked into the eyes of a cat, and a spark has been lit, and a flame of beauty has shone across a page. Here, of course, I must quote Blake's 'Tyger! Tyger! burning bright, in the forests of the night'. The word' burning', in such a context, is breath-taking—the quintessence of inspiration. It must have lit on Blake's pen like a flash of lightning from the night sky.

Every schoolboy knows the first couplet of the Tyger. (Even as I wrote this I was struck by the awful thought that there may be some horrid little creatures who do *not* know it.) But the rest of the poem may not be so familiar. The climax has always seemed to me to come in the fourth verse, after Blake has flung the immortal question 'In what distant deeps or skies, burnt the fire of thine eyes?'

What the hammer? What the chain?
In what furnace was thy brain?
What the anvil? What dread grasp
Dare its deadly terrors clasp?

Sometimes when I have been looking into the green mystery of 'Four's' eyes, and have marvelled at the way the dark band of the iris turns and thickens as he turns his head, I have seemed to see deeper and ever deeper, as though I were exploring some green corridor that stretched into infinity, and I have fancied that I caught a faint glow of red from Blake's furnace. But I have never been able to look long enough to make quite sure. 'Four' always stares me out, and compels me to lower my eyes. That is one very notable difference between dogs and cats. Often, if you stare into the eyes of a dog, he will look away in embarrassment, as though he knew that he was inferior. A cat will never do this. She will always stare back, because she knows that she is one's equal, if not one's superior.

Swinburne was one of the poets who noted this fact. Most of us only know Swinburne as the lyric virtuoso of his early poems, with their dazzling rhymes and alliterations ... poems in which there is always an echo of the sea, a tidal surge and a foam of spray. But he was in a very different mood when he wrote a poem to his cat.

> Stately, kindly, lordly friend
>   Condescend
> Here to sit by me, and turn
> Glorious eyes that smile and burn.
>
> Dogs may fawn on all and some
>   As they come
> You, a friend of loftier mind
> Answer friends alone in kind
> Just your foot upon my hand
> Softly bids it understand.

The non-F may interpret this charming verse as an attack on dogs. It is, of course, nothing of the sort. Swinburne was devoted to many dogs; he was merely observing that the cat is at least the dog's *social* superior. That is why the cat, unlike the dog, will always stare back at a human instead of lowering its eyes. The old saying that 'a cat may look at a queen' is sound natural history.

This proud gaze of the feline has been noted in a very moving poem by an English writer, Ruth Pitter. It is called 'To a Caged Lion', and the first verse runs ...

> You are afraid. You do not dare
> Up to the lion to lift your eyes,
> And unashamed his beauty share
> As once in that lost paradise.

Poet after poet has celebrated the strange aura of past glory that seems to glow round the heads of cats, the indefinable air of aristocracy, of ancient freedom, that makes one feel that there must be royal blood in the veins of even the scruffiest pussy in the alley. Many of the poets, too, have guessed that pussy is conscious of her heritage, and spends much of her life consoling herself for the sorrows of the present by recalling the splendours of the past. Time and again they invoke the image of the Sphinx, as in Baudelaire's *Les Fleurs du Mal* ...

Ils prennent en songeant les nobles attitudes
Des grands sphinx allongés au fond des solitudes
Qui semblent s'endormir dans un rêve sans fin.

However, most of our social intercourse with pussy is, fortunately, on not so lofty a level; otherwise we should be for ever bowing and curtseying to one another, and stepping back at doorways to offer precedence. That is why I think the poets rather overdo their favourite feline theme of the cat's ancient royal lineage. The theme is a true one, but it is not the only one, and sometimes poor pussy—starved, neglected, terrified by the cruelty of the world, is hard put to it to remember her royal antecedents.

Thomas Hardy must have realized this when he wrote a poem mourning the death of his own cat ... a poem which has a greater dignity and depth of feeling than many epitaphs for men and women.

From the chair whereon he sat
Sweep his fur, nor wince thereat;
Rake his little pathways out
Mid the bushes roundabout;
Smooth away his talons' mark
From the claw-worn pine-tree bark,
Where he climbed as dusk embrowned,
Waiting us who loitered round.

Strange it is this speechless thing
Subject to our mastering,
Subject for his life and food
To our gift, and time, and mood;
Timid pensioner of us Powers,
His existence ruled by ours,
Should—by crossing at a breath
Into safe and shielded death,
By the merely taking hence
Of his insignificance—
Loom as part, above man's will
Of the Imperturbable.

Strange indeed it is. Strange . . . and in some way comforting 'Safe and shielded death.' The last gift that not even the cruelty of man can deny.

W stands for Weaving.

'Weaving' is the name we give to charming curving movements which cats make round our legs when they are feeling more than usually friendly or when, to be frank, the fish is boiling and the kitchen is filled with a piscine aroma. I know of no other animal capable of performing these convolutions, which never fail to delight me—or perhaps I should have written, almost never, for there have been times when the weaving proclivities of 'Five' have made me late for a party. No sooner have I got into my dinner jacket than 'Five' appears, obviously drenched with affection, and sweeps round my legs, leaving my trousers covered with white and grey hair. 'You should not let him come near you when you are dressed for dinner,' says Gaskin severely, as he brushes my trousers. Which may be true but is not very helpful.

There are many varieties of Weaving, each with its special appeal. Some Fs, no doubt, prefer the Subtle Weave, which is executed with the delicacy of a gavotte. In this, the tail is held erect, and the human legs are scarcely touched. Others may have a preference for the Hind-Leg Weave, which explains itself with pussy rearing up and rubbing her neck against the legs. For myself, I most enjoy Butting Weave, and I like it to be executed with the greatest energy and enthusiasm. 'Five' is the supreme exponent of this type of weave; he butts his head against my legs as though he were playing football, darts away, turns and butts again; one would think he was trying to knock me down.

A moment ago I mentioned that one of the stimuli which induces a cat to weave is the aroma of boiling fish. This was perhaps an unwise remark, for it may be cited by the non-F as a proof of his familiar contention that feline affection is only cupboard love. 'A dog loves a man for himself, a cat only loves a man for what he can get out of him.' That is the argument, and a very ignorant and unjust argument it is.

Let us address a few words to the non-F in order that he may be better informed about dogs, cats and their respective capacities for affection. He is grossly misinformed if he assumes that cats love less deeply than dogs. Like a dog, a cat may die of a broken heart. But cats, being cats, are more subtle in the manner in which they manifest their feelings, and more selective in the choice of those persons on whom they bestow their favours. Most Fs will agree that to gain the love of a cat you must have, in yourself, some quality that is lovable.

Supposing that one owns a dog, and that one is returning home after a holiday. The dog will come running out in an ecstasy of joy, barking and leaping and fussing and sniffing, and it is all most endearing and satisfying. We all like to feel that somebody desires us, and to be desired so much, to be missed so passionately, is very flattering to the human ego.

With cats there is no such demonstration. On the contrary. Cats take a very different view of their owners' absences. They seem to feel themselves personally affronted. This is particularly the case with Siamese. Once, after I had been in America for a couple of months, I returned unexpectedly to find Gaskin out. My Siamese cat 'One' was lying on a chair in the hall. As soon as I entered he rose, cast upon me a look of withering scorn, stalked out into the conservatory, sat down on the mat, hoisted his leg, and proceeded to indulge in the intimacies of the toilet. '*That*,' he seemed to be saying, 'will teach you.'

I am not prone to putting words into the mouths of animals and I always feel embarrassed when charladies tell stories about their dogs or their cats, beginning with the words 'He looked at me, as much as to say . . .' However, on this occasion 'One' really did look at me 'as much as to say', and I fancy that I know what he was thinking. Something like this:

'So you have come home. And about time too! You need not imagine that you can come strolling back into my life, after weeks of neglect, and expect me to behave as though nothing had happened. Here have I been, all this time, carrying on the duties of the household, while you have been gadding about, enjoying yourself. I have worked my claws to the bone on your sofa. I have put in a great deal of work on the new curtains and I have demolished quantities of seed beds. I have sat for hours at the drawing-room window, studying the passers-by in the lane, and I have made quantities of notes. And all the time, you have been away. You have left it all to *me*. True, Gaskin has been the soul of courtesy and consideration, but that is not enough. No *sir*! This will all need very serious consideration before I decide upon my future attitude.'

A final touch to the toilet preparations, a last glance of scorn, and out stalks 'One' into the garden in the direction of the orchard into which he disappears with a sharp twitch of his tail. And it is not till nearly three days later, after a great deal of explanation on my part, and many hours of following him round the house, that at last he relents, allowing himself to be stroked, and rewards me with a purr.

Cats, in short, are the only animals who have mastered the art of sending their owners to Coventry—the only animals who know how to put us in our places. But if we behave ourselves, if we are regular in our attendance and if we avoid any of the grosser social errors, they are infinitely rewarding in their kindness.

How many times has my heart been cheered when I walk up the road of a summer evening and see, perched on the wall in the dusk, the familiar figure of 'Five' waiting to greet me. And how many times, when I have stroked him, has he begun to 'weave' with such enthusiasm that he has actually fallen off the wall. How many times, too, have I seen Oscar, sitting on the steps like a carven Sphinx . . . a Sphinx that suddenly comes to life and walks slowly towards me with the fading sunlight glinting in his eyes. And how many times, as I have bent down to savour the scent of the tobacco flowers, has a small black shape materialized from the shadows, and the quiet evening has heard the music of 'Four's' purr. These are the moments when we reap the richest rewards that come to the great family of Fs—moments of twilight and quietness, when we seem to speak the same language, and when we meet, as equals, in a world of peace.

X stands for ... well, X ... for all the imponderables and mysteries of the feline mind which were noted by Théophile Gautier. He was struck, in particular, by the curious affection which cats seemed to have for authors. He observed how frequently a cat will follow a writer into his study, and with what fascination it appears to regard his work, even to the extent of jumping on to his desk and endeavouring to seize his pen. In his memoirs of Baudelaire, Gautier wrote:

> They come to sit on the table by the writer, keeping his thoughts company, and gazing at him with intelligent tenderness and magical penetration. It seems as though cats divine the thought that is passing from the brain to the pen, and that as they stretch out a paw they are trying to seize it on its way.

Many non-Fs will tell you that they do not like cats because 'you never know what they are thinking'. This has always seemed to me a rather curious stricture, since it would serve with equal force as a reason for condemning the entire human race. However, non-Fs have never been noted for their logic.

X would seem a suitable section for a few words about the Sphinx who, as we have already observed, is so constantly evoked by the feline poets. When I was at school, I went through the usual period of decadence and fell for a while under the spell of Oscar Wilde whose poem 'The Sphinx' is literature's nearest approach to a Fabergé cigarette box. The spell did not last for long, probably because Wilde—though most people would disagree—was fundamentally non-F. It is not without interest to recall that one of the grossest examples in history of non-Fness was offered by the film production of *The Picture of Dorian Gray*. Hollywood, confronted with the task of adapting this curious fable to the taste of the average American schoolgirl, was in something of a quandary. Dr Kinsey had not yet lifted the veil on the private life of American undergraduates, and the Wolfenden Report was still lying, like a small unexploded bomb, in the womb of Time. So what did Hollywood do? The first thing, obviously, was to ensure that the role of Dorian was played by a young gentleman who would have been ideally cast as the captain of a football team. This was successfully arranged, and Dorian's languid epigrams were barked out, with obvious distaste, in tones that recalled the accents of a baseball coach. But this was not enough. Here was a story of evil and since Hollywood could not afford to admit the existence of *that* sort of evil, another victim must be found. So Hollywood chose the cat. In the centre of Dorian's fabulous apartment they placed a large statue of a cat, carved in the Egyptian manner. And whenever Dorian was moved by any of his illicit urges, and stamped his way out of the room, en route to nameless orgies, the cat was spot-lit, and the camera slowly tracked in to a close-up of it . . . as though the poor creature was at the root of the trouble. The suggestion, presumably, was that if only Dorian had invested in a nice cocker spaniel, all would have been well. This struck me as not only unbelievably stupid but vilely unjust, and caused me to give vent to a series of loud, sustained and faultlessly feline hisses, which eventually led to my removal from the cinema.

Wilde said that all men kill the thing they love; it would be truer to say that all men kill the thing they cannot understand. For instance, I have known non-Fs who were genuinely disturbed and discomfited by the sight of a cat staring out of a window. There it sits, confronted by apparent nothingness ... a blank wall, a deserted garden, or even a night of utter darkness. But the head darts backwards and forwards, the eyes are always intently focused, the tail lashes to and fro, and the whole body is rigid with interest. 'What is that wretched animal looking at?' asks the non-F uneasily. 'There is nothing to see. It gives me the creeps, going on like that about nothing.'

Which is foolish of the non-F. No living creature 'goes on like that about nothing'. I do not know if cats can really see in the dark; one imagines that some degree of light, however faint, is needed by even the exquisitely sensitive feline eyes. But obviously the cat is seeing *something*, some strange drama is being played out there, on that empty lawn, some mysterious shadow play is passing over that blank wall. Maybe the air is tingling with the echoes of some wild music from over the hills, to which our ears are deaf.

Y stands for Yawning.

Cats and dogs yawn in quite different ways and for quite different reasons. The yawn of a dog is seldom a sign of fatigue or of ennui; often it denotes intense excitement. A London friend of mine owns a small poodle which is perforce left alone in a flat for most of the day. Whenever I am able, I take it for a walk on Hampstead Heath. As soon as I open the door of the flat I am greeted with leaps of such hysterical delight that it is difficult to put Adolphus—for that is the dog's name—on the lead. This delight continues as we walk down the steps and enter the car. Never were there such extravagant demonstrations, such frenzied lickings, such curlings round on the seat, such leapings up to look through the window.

Then the car starts, and Adolphus sits still, quite rigid, staring at me with his pleasing poodle eyes. We are en route, yes, and that is all to the good, but why do we not go faster? Why must I sit at that silly wheel, staring through the glass, when ... so he seems to imagine ... I have only to open the door again to reveal the delights of the wide spaces of the Heath? Evidently he has not yet grasped the relation between time and distance; he does not realize that it takes a while to travel from point A to point B. So suddenly it comes, a long, dramatic yawn that seems to engulf his whole body. This is the absolute opposite of ennui, it is a trembling *cri de cœur*, an agonized protest at the cruel prolongation of his imprisonment.

No cat would ever carry on like that. Cats yawn for the sheer sensuous pleasure of it. And often, as they yawn, they arch their necks and stretch out their paws in front of them, as though to intensify that pleasure.

But Y stands for a great deal more than yawning. It is really a convenient device to introduce the whole fascinating subject of Sleep. (The letter 'S', as we have seen, was reserved for 'Stroking'.)

Even in their natural surroundings of the jungle, felines spend a very large proportion of their lives in sleep. This is a fact that offers a grain of consolation when one remembers how many of them have to live in captivity. Sometimes when I pass great blocks of modern flats I look up and think of all the cats and dogs and birds incarcerated behind those bleak façades. The thought would be almost unbearable if one did not remember that many of them, perhaps, were asleep. And even this thought would be unbearable if one did not believe that one day, when they died, they would wake to an eternal freedom.

Here is a problem that intrigues me; if you are a true F you have probably pondered it yourself. How is it that a cat who has slept through the winter months, week after week, for at least twenty hours out of the twenty-four, a cat who has partaken lavishly during this period of fish and milk, a cat whose only exercise has been to stretch on the carpet, to vault languidly on to the window sill and survey the rain-swept garden, to chatter its teeth for a few moments at the starlings and then to sink back into repose against the radiator

... how is it that such a creature, whom one would have thought to be flabby and utterly out of condition, can suddenly leap into life at the first sign of spring, shoot like an arrow across the lawn, and stream up the trunk of a tree as though it had spent the entire winter in training for the Olympic Games? (Reading over this question it seems the longest that even I have ever written. It would be agony to parse, and what we should have done without those three dots in the middle, I cannot imagine.)

But we will let the question stand. For it really is of interest. A human being who has slept so long and eaten so lavishly would be flabby and short of wind; his stomach would be distended, his muscles would be atrophied, and he would be hard put to it to climb a flight of stairs, let alone a tree. And yet pussy manages it with superb aplomb. Even 'Four', who as we have already observed is over eighty in human terms still leaps up the weeping-willow with the utmost grace, and perches on the top in the centre, where he looks like a sort of mad, black toque perched on the untidy head of a witch. One shudders to think of one's octogenarian acquaintances indulging in similar activities.

One of the myriad enchantments of living with cats lies in the fact that one never knows with whom one may be passing the night. Is one in favour? Will there be a small black shape ... 'Four' ... curled up on the foot of the bed? Or a plump black and white ball of fur ... 'Five' ... disposed primly in the middle? Or a huge, lean, mottled creature ... Oscar ... guarding the pillow?

Or will there be nobody at all? Will 'Four' have decided that the charms of the radiator exceed those of his master? Will 'Five' have deserted me for Gaskin? And will Oscar merely be absent, intent upon some mysterious errand in the shrubbery?

Sometimes, on gala nights, 'Four' and 'Five' both come to the conclusion that I am in need of nocturnal consolation. (Not Oscar, who never shares his favours.) Quite frankly, these occasions are not an unmixed delight. Naturally, one cannot dismiss them both; still less can one dismiss only one of them. To do so would be constructed as a sign of gross favouritism, and might set up a number of deep-rooted complexes. So one pretends to be enchanted, and slithers through the sheets, forcing a passage for one's body between 'Four' who is probably draped round one's ankles, and 'Five', who reclines like an enormous furry hot-water-bottle in the crook of one's knees. And then one turns out the light and hopes for the best ... hopes that one will not get cramp, that 'Four' will not decide that he would be more comfortable on one's stomach, that 'Five' will not hear the owl hooting outside and jump up and scratch at the door to be let out, and that the soft duet of purrs will slowly lull one to sleep.

An awful thought has suddenly assailed me. I have just remembered the young woman from Bexhill-on-Sea.

She is the very last person whom I should have wished to remember, at a tranquil moment like this, but since she has intruded herself, she must be dealt with ... severely. For all I know, there may be others like her, lurking in sea-side resorts around our coasts.

About a year ago, this young woman who lives at Bexhill-on-Sea wrote me a very rude letter out of the blue. Apparently she has heard that I sometimes have cats sleeping on my bed at night, and the information disgusted her. 'Of all the unhygienic habits!!!' she exclaimed. (She was one of those correspondents whose pen spouts exclamation marks.) 'How *can* you? If I ever had any children I should punish them severely if I ever caught them with cats on their beds!!! What about the *germs*?' To which one might retort that if she felt so strongly about germs in bed she would probably never have any children at all. I would swop the entire microbic content of 'Four' and 'Five' for that of one energetic young sanitary inspector.

This letter from Bexhill-on-Sea not only angered but astonished me, because I happen to be President of the Bexhill-on-Sea Cat Club, which is a highly geared, streamlined organization, with a powerful influence in the concerns of that resort. I have been given to understand that the favour of the Bexhill-on-Sea Cat Club is eagerly sought—as it should be—by persons aspiring to seats on the local council, and that those upon whom it frowns have little chance of achieving eminence. In so civilized a locality one would have thought that there would be no place for young women with such grossly incorrect notions about cats sleeping on beds. Evidently one was wrong, and something must be done. One must Use One's Influence.

And that will be enough for the young lady from Bexhill-on-Sea.

Now for a word about cats' sleeping quarters. In their choice of couches cats show an exquisite ingenuity. They reveal themselves as domestic sybarites, with an uncanny facility for finding the warmest quarters of the house, and as jungle realists, who are never forgetful of the dangers of sudden attack. True, in a normal household this danger is seldom more acute than the sudden onslaught of the daily woman with carpet-sweeper. (I have spoken to Gaskin dozens of times about that daily woman but she still comes. She is enough to drive one mad. She stands in the middle of the music-room in a sort of trance, pushing the carpet-sweeper up and down as though she were fanning herself. When she is not doing this she is drinking such enormous quantities of tea that one's own stomach shudders in sympathy. The cats hate her, and I hate her, and I cannot believe that those rattling carpet-sweepers do any good. But she still comes. However, this is a domestic 'aside' that will probably be struck out in the proofs.[1])

To return to this bed business. Let me tell you about the most beautiful bed in the whole world, which once belonged to 'Five'. This was the linen cupboard at Merry Hall—my old house that has gone with the wind. It was a haven of warmth, and quiet, and peace and utter security. Tell me if you can imagine any sweeter place of repose. You walked up an old Georgian staircase, with the sunlight slanting through the delicate slits of the balustrade. Ahead of you was 'Five', with his bushy tail very erect, for pleasure was in store, and sleep, in such perfect surroundings as he anticipated, would be not merely a passive abandonment of care, it would be an active pleasure. You passed down a corridor and 'Five's' tail switched to the right, into a shadowy little alcove which concealed the entrance to the linen cupboard. There was a faint mew, a glint of green eyes as 'Five' looked up at you, and the gentle extension of a paw. Then

[1]As you will observe, it was not. The woman has been struck out instead.

you opened the door, and the haven of the linen cupboard was revealed.

Haven, indeed, it was. Warm, roomy, dark, mysterious—but mysterious in a way that breathed a strange friendliness. Shelf upon shelf of sheets and blankets and pillow-slips, with here and there an eiderdown or a bed cover that had faded, and in the top left-hand corner a patchwork quilt. Everything was well worn and familiar, and some of the sheets would soon be sent to the laundry for the last time. But everything proclaimed peace.

And then, 'Five' would spring up on to the first shelf, pausing for a moment to stick his tail up and indulge in a few delicate kneading movements with his paws. Then over and up to the second shelf, and the third, which was the elevation that most suited him. Whereupon he would turn round and round with great fastidiousness between an old pink blanket and a quilt and a couple of ancient curtains, until finally he had made a 'nest'. (My mother once told me that the reason why cats turned round in circles before lying down to sleep was because they remembered the old days in the jungle, when they had to flatten down the long grasses in order to make a bed. My mother had a large store of these charming little tit-bits of science. I see no reason why they should not be true.)

So now the picture is complete, with 'Five' in his nest, and his green eyes glinting in the semi-darkness, and the gentle warmth of the radiators creeping up to soothe him. And now, too, I remember that this section comes under Y. So we will allow him the luxury of a last Yawn, and close the door—or rather, leave it ajar—and tiptoe away.

Z stands for . . .

Whatever else we may decide that Z stands for, it does not stand for Zoos. This is a book in which no institution so miserable as a Zoo should play any part. I am totally unable to understand the general public's attitude to Zoos. There are thousands of normal kindly women with cats and dogs of their own—women who would be outraged if they were accused of cruelty, who nevertheless see nothing in the least objectionable in seizing wild animals, dragging them from their natural environment and incarcerating them for life—for *life*, mind you—in cages so small that they can hardly turn. Not only do these people see nothing wrong in this practice but they take their horrible children to glare at the animals, and giggle and throw buns and poke sticks. And then, having thoroughly warped and perverted their infants' minds they express astonishment when their darlings grow up to be 'juvenile delinquents' . . . which is the modern euphemism for immature thugs.

I have—and so, I imagine, have you—a number of favourite day-dreams, though day-dreams is not quite the right expression, as I usually indulge them at twilight. There is the day-dream when I am a millionaire, able to employ innumerable slaves in creating the perfect garden, waving a hand and saying: 'Let there be balustrades and terraces and foundations, and kindly cover the entire slopes of that

hill over with daffodils . . . *at once*.' (There have been several occasions in the past, when I have forgotten that this was a day-dream, and have begun to put the idea into practice, which is the reason why I shall probably end up in an old gentlemen's home.) There is another day-dream where I have a sort of magic box which emits incredibly powerful and mysterious rays, rather like the instruments of destruction which figure so largely in space fiction. In this dream I float gaily round the world, turning my rays on to persons who seem to be more than usually objectionable at the moment—dictators, child-beaters and sadists in general. During the rape of Hungary my box was in such constant and concentrated use that it is a wonder there were any rays left in it. But there were and . . . I warn you . . . there still are.

But in my favourite day-dream of all, reserved for very special occasions, when the twilight is lit with a magic glow and the psychic influences are at their most powerful, I have discovered a secret key that unlocks all the cages at the Zoo. And I tiptoe through the entrance, and turn all the locks and fling open all the gates, beginning of course at the smaller cat section. And there is a roaring and a raging and a gnashing of teeth and a flashing of wild, accusing eyes. And the animals rush past me and leap over the railings, and flood the highways and byways of northern London in a vast avenging stream. They crash through the windows of respectable parlours and descend on plump families watching television and send their teeth crunching through the fat bottoms of the ladies who, for so many years, have been insulting them with buns. They pick up overfed little boys with a single, exquisite gesture and hurl them over the roof. They pounce on prosperous city men, rip off their clothes, and propel them like ping-pong balls into the icy waters of the Regent's Canal. And then licking their lips, purring ferociously—but far from satisfied—they depart *en masse*, to deal with the directors.

You must admit that this is a most pleasing day-dream, and I should feel comforted if I thought that you might sometimes indulge it. If enough people dream the same dream, there is always the chance that one day it might come true.

* * *

This is perhaps a jarring note on which to end this alphabet, which has been written mainly in accordance with the legend engraved on ancient sundials . . . 'I count only the sunlit hours.' But all Fs will agree with me that if one loves animals one has to pay for it, and that the pains and sorrows of the animal world can wring our hearts as acutely as any of the woes of mankind. Sometimes, when I have come across some animal in distress and when—as so often—I have been tragically incompetent to do anything about it, I have wished that there were some sort of pill which one could swallow, to numb the heart and steel the brain against pity. Anti-Pity Pills would make life simpler in a hundred ways, and I greatly envy the number of persons who appear to have access to an unlimited supply of them.

Failing such a potion, the best one can do, in order that life should not be one long heart-ache, is to try to be intelligent. Above all, to avoid the emotional snares of excessive anthropomorphism. To credit an animal with the same pains and fears as one feels in one's own body is, I think, unjustified. (At least, I very much hope so!) Obviously, there are degrees of pain, and it is not unreasonable to suppose that they vary in intensity according to the sensitivity of the sufferer. A migraine in the brain of a Shelley or Mozart, one imagines, would be more agonizing than in the brain of an all-in wrestler. Going down the scale, the wrestler might suffer more acutely than the Australian aboriginal, who in his turn might suffer more than the chimpanzee, who has a more delicate nervous system than the bulldog and so on almost *ad infinitum*, until we come down to the lowest form of animal life, the sea anemone on the rocks. This, at least, is how I try to comfort myself when I see a lost kitten. I tell myself that it is not really so bad as if it were a lost baby.

And yet, even with sea anemones, it distresses me when small boys poke their fingers into them and bruise them, and make them close their delicate, waving limbs. After all, sea anemones *are* a form of life and a very beautiful form of life; they must experience some form of joy and delight on their secret rocks, with the green waters drifting over them, and the sunlight filtering through. Equally they must experience some form of terror and dismay when they are brutally assaulted.

I am well aware that these are unfashionable sentiments which, to many, will appear absurd. I have served, too often, as a target for ridicule to be unaware of the rich gift which I am handing to the satirist. 'Humanity in peril of extinction . . . and Nichols drools about sea anemones!' That is one obvious line of attack. It does not greatly concern me. There is a reverse side to every argument, and it might not be unreasonable to suggest that if more people began to concern themselves with such humble creatures as sea anemones they might, as they ascended the ladder of life, show more consideration for humanity. In any case, it is not so very intelligent to despise the sea anemones; they were our original ancestors and after we have reaped the whirlwind they may, once again, be the only form of life that stirs in the waters of an empty world.

Which reminds me that it is time to give the cats their fish. For the past twenty minutes there have been restless movements in the corridor, the sound of impatient scratchings on the carpet, and even heads protruding round the edge of my study door. So I will lay down my pen and attend to more important business. You remember the routine? 'Four' under the kitchen sink, 'Five' on the table, and Oscar by the side of the dresser. When I think of such pleasant little domestic conventions I feel that life, after all, has a pattern, and makes some sort of sense.

A stands for Autumn.

There had been a sharp frost in the night, the first of the season, and when I went out into the garden after breakfast the little golden acacia at the far end of the lawn was standing in a circle of fallen yellow leaves, like a young girl who had just stepped out of a silken dress. Near by the liquidambars were so thickly hung with frosted cobwebs that their twigs seemed to be *diamanté*, and I remember thinking that they were really rather overdressed . . . all those jewels at so early an hour. (Which reminds me of a very rich acquaintance whom I once surprised in the herbaceous border, pulling up groundsel, which of course is the nicest weed to pull up. She was wearing a smock of expensive simplicity and a beautiful pearl necklace. I made some remark about the necklace and she replied, quite casually and with no trace of affectation. 'Oh ... these are my gardening pearls.' In spite of this she is an an agreeable woman and fundamentally F[1].)

But we were talking of autumn. There I was, standing on the lawn, not only looking but listening, to one of the most magical echoes in the whole symphony of nature, the sound of falling leaves. They were falling from the branches of the old walnut tree that stretched its gnarled branches over the outbuildings, and the morning was so hushed that one heard each leaf distinctly as it fell, sighing and fluttering through the misty air. It would be pleasant, I thought, if we could all leave the world in so graceful a fashion; at one moment high up in the branches of an old tree, and then—a sudden feeling of fatigue, a swift farewell and a gentle parting, knowing, as we left the parent branch, that even now, though a new life awaited us, it would be a life of growth and service.

And then, the silence was broken by a cough behind me. I looked round and saw 'Four', the eldest of my three cats. He was sitting on the yellow leaves of the acacia, and he looked very black, very cold, and very pathetic. He coughed again.

Now it must be explained that 'Four', in case this is the first time that you have met him, is the Cat Who Does the Act. A fuller interpretation of this title will be found under 'Jealousy'. For the moment it is enough to say that at a very early age 'Four' decided that he would be most likely to obtain a lion's share of the good things of life if he adopted a role in which he appeared to be persecuted and maltreated. He has never, to my knowledge, received even the mildest of slaps, but if he is not getting his own way in every respect he will immediately register an expression of terror, and retreat with such alarm and dismay that anybody witnessing this little drama immediately leaps to the conclusion that I am a cat-beater.

Coughing is part of the Act. It is usually employed if the fish is not served precisely to his liking. 'Four' bends over the plate, sniffs, turns round, and then—always provided that he has an audience—

[1]A note on the correct interpretation of Fness and non-Fness will be found in the Foreword, in case it has escaped your attention.

goes straight into the Act with a positive Mimi of a cough. The assumption, of course, is that he is a poor, neglected creature, rapidly heading for a decline, whose demise can only be averted by a swiftly opened tin of tongue. It is all very professionally timed and executed, and the only reason it is not quite heart-rending is that 'Four', like many other Mimis whom one has seen expiring in Act Four of *La Bohème*, is exceedingly plump.

Still, one never knew. 'Four' *might* have a real cough. After all, he was getting on, like others who shall be nameless. There had been a worrying week, three years ago, when he had bronchitis. I bent down, picked him up, and gently felt the tip of his nose. Oh dear ... it was hot. And 'Four' usually has a nose as cold as an icicle.

So here we went again. Away from the falling leaves, away from the peace of the garden, and back to the house with 'Four' snuggling in our arms, to seek out Gaskin, who would know what to do.

B stands for Backwater.

Without any great effort on our part, the stage of this little revue seems to have set itself—the high-walled garden adrift with falling leaves. And two of the main characters have introduced themselves—'Four', the eldest of our feline trio, and Gaskin, the factotum and friend of many years. Now that 'Four' is safely in Gaskin's arms—'I knew that this would happen; he *will* sit right in the stove in the draught of the cat-door'—we can briefly introduce the two other principal players, 'Five' and Oscar.

Both are tabbies, but there the resemblance ends. 'Five,' who does not eat excessively, is round and very plump; Oscar, who eats like a horse, remains lean and lanky. 'Five', in spite of his plumpness, is something of a cynic, and plays 'hard to get'. This, I suspect, is due to the fact that when he was a baby he was chased all over the house by a Pekinese and ended up by jumping on to the lawn from a high window . . . one of those moments in one's life one would prefer to forget. (Whenever I hear people saying 'Of course, cats can fall from *any* height without hurting themselves' I feel like retorting 'Quite. And if a woman is silly enough you can pour boiling oil down her neck without her even noticing it.')

Where were we? Oh yes . . . 'Five', and his cynicism. Oscar, on the other hand, has no trace of cynicism; he is a pushover, mentally and physically, for anybody who shows him affection. And since most of my friends are firmly F, he spends a great deal of his life flopping on to his back, with his front paws dangling, demanding chin-strokings and tummy-rubbings. And, in the case of exceptionally advanced Fs, reversed whisker-strokings.[1]

'Four', 'Five' and Oscar having made their brief bows, in their respective fashions, I should like to 'pan back', as I believe they say in the movie studios, and take a wider view, so that we may see our little house as though it were on a large-scale map, with the various neighbouring cats marked with a cross. However, since this section has already run to an inordinate length, let us move on.

My cottage is situated on Ham Common, in the county of Surrey, and perhaps some people might quarrel with the description of such a locality as a 'backwater'. They would point out that only three miles to the north is the flourishing county town of Richmond, through which the traffic pours to the sea-coast. And that three miles to the south is the equally flourishing county town of Kingston ... to say nothing of the crowds that throng Hampton Court throughout the summer.

However, certain parts of England have a strange magic which might be described as a quality of withdrawal; they seem to turn into backwaters in their own right. And just as in the City of London you may suddenly step from the traffic's roar into a courtyard as hushed and tranquil as Magdalene College in the Long Vacation, so, in the neighbourhood of my cottage, you have only to walk a few yards to find yourself in the heart of the country.

I open the front door, sniff the sweet air, and the even sweeter lemon-verbena which flourishes by the porch. I turn to the left, past the cottages of my neighbours, which like my own were built in the year 1800 and look exactly like a setting for one of Jane Austen's novels. At the end of the row, an exquisite Queen Anne house looms into view, a fairy-tale house whose name is ... but let

[1] A note on reversed whisker-stroking will be found in a later section. It demands a very high standard of technique, and may be compared, pianistically, with the cadenza in the eleventh section of Rachmaninoff's Paganini Variations. It should not be attempted by amateurs.

us keep some mystery in these pages. I shall call it the Great House, and I shall name its charming young owners Lord and Lady X. And I shall indulge myself in dreams of future days when, as an extremely impoverished and decrepit author, I sit by a starveling fire, polishing my crutches, and Lady X knocks on the door with a bowl of soup.

These painful scenes have not yet materialized. Lady X has indeed knocked on the door, but the last time she did so it was to borrow a lemon from Gaskin because somebody had unexpectedly sent them a tin of caviare.

I want to linger for a few more moments in front of the Great House. It is all part of the feline setting; 'Four', 'Five', and Oscar often visit it, via the garden walls, though I do not think that as yet they have formally left their cards. Most days of my life I wander past it, on my way to the silver birch woods, and always I pause, peopling it with the ghosts who must still tenant it. Sometimes I think I see the pale frustrated face of Mrs Fitzherbert, staring out of one of the windows in the west wing, cursing the rain-swept common to which she had been banished when her fortunes were at their lowest ebb. But always I see the bent, shabby figure of Daniel Defoe, ambling his way across the lawn to vanish in the shadows of the giant cedars. For it was from the bricks of Defoe's little factory on the Thames that the Great House was built. The author of *Robinson Crusoe* was probably the first professional writer, and certainly not the last, who found it necessary to augment his income by taking jobs 'on the side'.

None of which, as you may well remind me, has anything to do with cats.

But I am trying to set the scene, to give you the feeling of the backwater. Cats, like many other animals, need a landscape that is hushed, a landscape in which they can hear all the thrilling natural sounds of challenge and alarm—the challenge of the woodpecker, tapping on the walnut tree, the alarm that comes when the wind rattles the door of the tool-shed as though one of the hated dustmen had knocked it with his elbow.

And our landscape is indeed hushed. For beyond the Great House the woods begin, my favourite kind of woods, all silver birch and bracken. And beyond the woods are the wide, rolling expanses of Richmond Park, with the wild deer playing. A man may well lose himself in Richmond Park, as I know from tiresome experience. And beyond the Park . . . admittedly . . . lies London. But I have always felt that it is really a very long way off, in a completely different world, that it lacks all substance. If you stand on one of the little hills of the Park you can see London in the distance, but it looks as though it were the backcloth to a child's theatre, all tinsel and cardboard, and you can cock a snook at it. You need not be frightened by it—as sane men must be frightened by all cities. (Any-

body who can look at the Empire State Building without a feeling of alarm and despair must be, *ipso facto*, nuts.) Here in the Park you are safe, with your feet on the sweet, soft turf, and the wild deer grazing, and the venerable oaks lifting their arms in perpetual prayer to an untainted sky.

That is our background. And if this were a different kind of opus I could meander about in it for ever. But as this is a scientific work, written with an eye to the veterinary surgeon book-reading public—which I gather is enormous, and largely untapped—we must reluctantly leave the Park, and wander home through the silver birch woods to Ham Common.

Which brings us to the next section

C stands for Cottage.

When we have done with this section, the scene will be finally set.

One of the nicest things that ever happened to me was when the President of the Royal Academy suddenly arrived at the cottage on a hot Sunday afternoon, stumped out into the middle of the lawn, demanded a paper and pencil, and began to draw. And then, when he had made a number of enchanting sketches of eaves and windows and porticoes, turned to me with a little smile and said:

'This is a Jane Austen house; this is a *tender* house.'

No doubt many members of the Virile School of Modern Prose, wielding their pens with a force that might be more suitably employed for the harpooning of whales, would resent the suggestion that they lived in a 'tender' house. To me, the adjective is apposite and consoling, particularly when I recall the distinction of the man who made it—a man who is among the most considerable architects of our age.

How can we convey this 'tenderness'? Perhaps we might begin at the front door. This looks out on to a pocket-handkerchief of a garden—the main garden, of course, is at the back—which I have deliberately kept as 'cottagey' as possible. The white latticed porch (*circa* 1800) could hardly be prettier. It screamed for a honeysuckle and got it, and if I knew a very old lady, permanently wrapped in shawls, with a penchant for sitting in porches, I should hire her by the hour. Just by the porch there is the aforesaid lemon-verbena, for crunching and sniffing purposes on one's exits and entrances. (It is heart-rending to think that there must be quite large numbers of people who have to go to work every morning without the soothing anodyne of a pinch of lemon-verbena; one cannot imagine how they get through the day.) The path up to the porch is lined, needless to say, with lavender. There is a raised bed in the centre for wall-flowers in the spring and pinks in the summer, which cluster round the feet of a little eighteenth-century statue in lead—a boy playing a flute. I am always afraid that one day somebody will come and steal him, but I have put such appalling curses on anybody who might do so, and woven such hideous spells against any possible marauder, that the atmosphere round the figure is probably charged with sufficient menace to act as a deterrent.

Add a shrub of rosemary in one corner, a clump of madonna lilies in another, a row of floribunda roses under the white railings, and you have the front garden.

Let us step inside.

Ahead of us is a narrow staircase, with a simple but elegant balustrade of pitch pine. We can now remind ourselves that this is supposed to be a book about cats, for it is fairly certain that 'Five' will be reposing on the sixth step. (He chooses the sixth step because there is a hot water pipe concealed in the wall behind it.) He lies at full length, with his tail dangling down, and since the step is narrow and 'Five' is inclined to be plump, he slightly bulges over the edge. He is something of an obstacle to traffic between the two floors, but he is never disturbed. Or almost never. We once had a very disagreeable daily woman who was afflicted—probably rightly—by rheumatism, and one day she was discovered pushing 'Five' out of the way with her foot. It need hardly be said that her reign came to an abrupt conclusion and for a short time the spells and curses which were normally used for the protection of the little boy in the front garden were transferred, with increased vehemence, in her direction.

We open a door on the left and—minding the step—we enter the principal room in the house. This, of course, is the music-room. Where the piano is, there is one's treasure, as far as I am concerned. It is long, low room which was formerly two, looking out on to the lawn. Today it is white and sunny and sparkling, but when I first saw it my heart sank; it was so dark that even on the brightest of mornings one would have to turn on the electric light before one could play the piano. This would be intolerable, for nothing, surely, is more delightful than sitting down at the piano on a summer day, and playing Chopin or Debussy while the natural sunlight drifts over one's shoulders through the vines outside, creating a filigree of shadow on the printed page ... a shifting pattern of ghostly leaf and blossom that dances to the mood of the music.

The main cause of this darkness came from a giant copper beech whose sombre arms stretched right over the roof, and I had not been in residence for a couple of days before my heart was sinking lower than ever, for two reasons.

Firstly, because I knew that the copper beech would have to come down and because it is hateful to destroy a beautiful tree.

Secondly, because the cottage was Crown property, and because the lease contained a clause that no tree could be cut down without the permission of the Crown Commissioners.

Having a somewhat vivid imagination I immediately transformed the Commissioners, in my mind's eye, into evil implacable monsters with horns, whose sole purpose in life was to condemn me to perpetual darkness. It never occurred to me, for one moment, that they might in fact be normal human beings, amenable to reason. When Gaskin suggested that I should write to them and explain the situation I could hardly believe my ears. How could he make such an astonishing proposal? How *could* one write to such creatures? Where did they live? . . . What did they look like? Did Gaskin know? Of course not. Nobody knew anything about the Crown Commissioners. All one knew, with certainty, was that they had horns, that they spent their lives plotting misery for people like myself. And that they were not in the telephone book.

So months were wasted trying to devise means by which we could rid ourselves of the copper beech without the knowledge, let alone the assistance, of the hated Crown Commissioners. We tried the most powerful spells and incantation, without effect. We got up in the small hours of the morning and crawled along the wall, and nipped off small branches here and there, but the more we nipped the more gigantic the tree seemed to become. To tackle the problem in this manner would take years and obviously, before we had finished it, the horned ones would be upon us. One night, in a local pub, I talked loudly and despairingly of my affliction, in the mood of Henry II when he cried for the death of Thomas Becket. 'Who will rid me of this pestilent beech?' I demanded. On the following morning I was called upon by an exceptionally sinister youth of seafaring origin, who had overheard the conversation. He had a touch of the tar-brush, and 'I love Mum' tattooed across the knuckles of his left hand, which is always a bad sign. He told me that he was an expert in poisoning trees, and as he was quite obviously an expert in poisoning practically anything, I showed him the door. A moment later, in a state of nervous prostration, I was ringing up the Crown Commissioners. They *were* in the telephone book, after all.

A few days later 'they' came down, in the shape of a nice young man in a bowler hat, which, when removed, betrayed no trace of horns. He refused the outsize dry martinis which I offered him in order that he might be stunned into a mood of acquiescence. He paced round the copper beech, he went in and out of the house, he examined the walls, went into the house again, talked to Gaskin, came back. For a moment I had a terrible feeling that he might have horns after all. Then he delivered his decision. Of course the copper beech must come down. It was not only darkening the house and impoverishing the garden, it was getting into the drains.

So down it came, one bright July morning, with a thud that shook the earth like a giant fist and set all the dogs barking for miles around.

And I had all the usual feelings of remorse and self-reproach when I saw the proud branches humbled and withering. But the cottage breathed a sigh of relief; it was almost as though you could see the lattice windows blinking and opening their eyes to the light that had so long been denied them.

This book is getting out of hand. There are cats to the right of us, cats to the left of us, purring, mewing, scratching in the wings, but I cannot seem to get them on the stage. All because I am taking so long in hanging the backcloth.

But please bear with me for a few more pages. Cats make such exquisite entrances that they deserve a proper setting. If a Siamese cat were to appear at the top of the staircase in the Savoy Hotel, and slowly, haughtily descend to the main dining-room, tail erect, all the women would be put to shame. The dowagers would retreat to the Ladies' and then go home. The more intelligent of the models, it is hoped, would take out their pencils, and make notes.

So we must go back to the music-room, into which the light is now flooding, after the decease of the copper beech, flooding and streaming in aqueous ripples of light that flicker round the fireplace and over the keys of the piano.

But the room was still not light enough. Cottage rooms, however picturesque, very seldom are. So I devised a plan which, in its turn, led to a story. And when I have told it, the cats at last can take the stage. We will call it . . .

THE STORY OF THE THREE MIRRORS

It happened like this. My plan for the music-room was very simple—to cover the darkest wall with squares of old mirror which would echo the sunlight and bring the sparkle of life to a moribund corner. In case you think that mirrored walls are reminiscent of bathrooms in smart hotels, I can assure you that this was not the idea at all. The effect I wanted was more like a tapestry of faded silver. All the pieces of glass would have to be old and softened by the fingers of time, and they would have to blend into the wall as though they had hung there for ever.

So I sent for Mr Barnes, the local builder, otherwise known as Hamlet. We have called him Hamlet because whenever a job is suggested to him he sighs deeply, folds his arms, and steps aside, wrapped in melancholy, and stares at whatever has to be done, soliloquizing. I can never quite catch what he is saying; it is probably only something to do with paint and plaster; but the sighs are so profound, and his features are so sicklied o'er with the pale cast of thought, that the effect is most moving. When I told him about the mirror idea, he was literally shaken with sighs, and he began to murmur with more than usual emotion. In the end, however, it transpired that he was only making notes about the nature of the frame that would be needed to support the pieces of glass. He suggested that I should advertise for old mirrors in the *Richmond and Twickenham Times*.

Which I did. And in due course I received a number of replies, most of them unhelpful and one of them, to put it mildly, bizarre. It might be thought that an advertisement for old-fashioned mirrors would be the last thing to evoke any suggestion of impropriety, but this was obviously the effect that it had on a certain elderly gentleman living on the outskirts of Twickenham. From his letter I gathered that as a young man in the Navy he had spent a number of riotous nights in a certain glittering establishment in Marseilles, where the ladies could be watched from behind specially treated transparent mirrors, without realizing that they were being observed. One of these mirrors he had annexed, and he offered to sell it to me. I am not a great expert on these matters, and though I have often heard of trick mirrors I have never been quite clear about who watches whom or who sees what . . . let alone why anybody bothers to do either. So I did not answer the letter. But I could not help thinking that it must be rather mournful, after a youth of such sauciness, to end one's days as an old gentleman on the outskirts of Twickenham, with nothing to look at but one's own face.

That is the curious story of the first mirror. An equally curious episode is recalled by the second. It came from a little pub in Hampton—one of those modest inns where you feel the customers are all members of a big family. I called out of business hours and was greeted at the side door by an immensely fat lady with marigold hair, cerise lips, and so much costume jewellery that she could have furnished a Christmas tree without missing anything.

The woman gave me a jolly smile, said 'pleased to meet you', and led me through the empty bar to a large shed at the back, that was filled with a clutter of junk. There, leaning against the wooden wall, was a large mirror, six foot by six, just what I wanted, with a nice dim patina. She asked only three pounds for it, which I paid her on the spot. When the bargain was completed, she turned and looked back at her reflection—a grotesque, monstrous, unnaturally swollen reflection—hung with all those baubles.

'In a way I'll be sorry to let it go.' There was a catch in her voice. 'When I was training for the ballet I used to do my exercises in front of that old mirror. Dreamed of doing *Swan Lake*, I did.' She forced a smile, and threw up her head, trying for a moment to defeat her double chins. Then she sagged back to normal. 'Some Swan!' She gave me a rather sad little wink, and led the way out.

The last mirror was leaning against a wall in the parlour of a small shabby house that stood on a backwater of the Thames. You could see the river running in it, deep and silent, like a green ribbon fluttering over the silver surface. If you had been standing by my side you would also have seen its owner—a little woman in black, who spoke in a low, sweet voice. Years ago, she must have been as pretty as they come, and even now her cheeks had the clear pink of wild roses—a pink that flushed gently as she spoke:

'I am afraid it is not in very good condition,' she was saying. 'You can see for yourself; the frame is badly chipped, and there is a crack right across the centre.'

'I shan't be using the frame. And it doesn't matter about the crack, because I shall be cutting it up.'

'Cutting it up?' She glanced at me, and for a moment I thought she was going to make some protest. Then she looked back in the mirror and nodded to herself. 'I see.'

'I hope you won't mind that.'

'It will hardly be my concern when I have sold it.' She went on staring into the mirror. 'It is just that it has sentimental associations.'

Suddenly I realized that she was acutely lonely, and that she was longing to talk to somebody . . . anybody . . . before the mirror went out of her life.

Then she told me the story—the simplest and most hackneyed of stories, but for some reason it moved me deeply. It happened over fifty years ago, at the beginning of the First World War, when the shabby little house had not been so shabby, when the garden had not been rank and overgrown, and when trim lawns had stretched down to the river, lawns on which there were elegant tea-parties, and young men who had danced attendance—young men who, as the summer, faded, changed from their white flannels into the khaki that was to become the sombre habit of a doomed generation. Among these young men was one in particular who fell in love with her, and she with him. He came to say goodbye on March 15, 1915. Why I recall that date I do not know—perhaps because the old lady remembered it herself so intensely. He went out by the front door, and she came back to the parlour, to be by herself, to think, to try to be brave. Then she heard a tap on the window. She looked up and there he was reflected in the mirror, smiling and waving; he had walked round the house for a last glimpse of her.

'He walked backwards, over the lawn, waving and smiling. I waved too, but I was crying, and I did not want him to see, so I turned away again, and watched him in the mirror.' Her voice was quite calm . . . there was even the shadow of a smile on her own face. 'I remember that the crocuses were out, and I was afraid that he would step on them. But he noticed them, just in time.'

She never saw him again. He was killed a week later.

At length the two mirrors were delivered, together with a number of other strips and pieces, all of which had their own stories which there is no space to tell. And when I sit at the piano, and play the music that I love, by sunlight, by candlelight, in the dusk of an April evening, the silvered wall that faces me seems like the backcloth of a tiny theatre that is peopled by ghosts . . . the ghosts of the wicked ladies of Marseilles, the ghost of a young dancer, laughing and flicking her fingers, and the ghost of a girl standing at a window, waving,

with tears in her eyes, tears which misted the gold of the crocuses. 'I was afraid that he would step on them.'

So now at last the scene is set—enough of it for our purpose. And to assure you that this indeed is going to be a book about cats, I may mention that all the cats, in their various ways, were deeply interested in the mirrored wall as soon as it was completed. Oscar was inclined to be skittish with it, and dabbed at himself. 'Five', who has Narcissus tendencies, sat in front of it and stared into his own green eyes for such long periods that when he eventually tore himself away he looked quite dopey. It was left to 'Four' to pretend that the mirrors were hostile and full of baneful influences. And so, although he is an elderly and quite sophisticated cat who knows all about mirrors, he would stroll innocently past the wall and then—always provided that he had an audience—register sudden terror, and slink away, glancing backwards as though Coleridge's fearful fiend were treading close behind him.

D stands for Drawers.

Let us hasten to explain that this chapter is in no way concerned with ladies' and gentlemen's underwear. The drawers to which we refer belong to bureaux, tallboys, and such-like. As soon as we have opened them, pussy, by some mysterious instinct, is aware of what we are up to, and appears from nowhere, in order leap into the drawers, inspect their contents, and if necessary curl up and go to sleep on them.

I have a few decent pieces of furniture. One of them is a walnut tallboy which I bought from an old gentleman called Mr Crowther who lived in an astonishing blend of splendour and confusion at Syon Lodge, surrounded by acres of exquisite temples, urns, cherubs, fountains, and Regency commodes, which he sold at erratic prices to the nobility and gentry ... and occasionally to people such as myself. (I say 'erratic' because if he liked you he took ten per cent off the bill and if he didn't he put ten per cent on.)

Back to the tallboy. Forty pounds it was, and it should have been eighty. There it stands in my bedroom, slim and elegant, and you would not think that it had any psychic qualities. But it must have some power of communication, for as soon as I open one of its drawers, particularly if it is a drawer containing some newly laundered dress shirts, Oscar appears from nowhere, and either leaps

into it unasked or—if it is too high—demands in no uncertain terms that he should be lifted up and put inside.

Fs will agree that these demands should be granted, though on wet days, when pussy has just come in from the garden, it is first permissible to sponge the paws and wipe them dry. For some reason which I have never been able to fathom, the drawer containing the dress shirts is always the favourite, although it is at the top and shallower than the rest of them, and although the shirts are covered in cold, crackly Cellophane. One would have thought that the bottom drawer, which is much more commodious and is comfortably lined with socks and woollen pullovers, would have been more popular. But no—the top drawer it must be, and there Oscar sits, purring and crackling, with his large square, whiskered face protruding over the edge. If I slightly close the drawer, which he seems to like, he looks like some strange Cheshire cat in one of Alice's unrecorded adventures.

I have often wondered if this almost universal feline desire to curl up in drawers is an example of the Return-to-the-Womb complex—which, once one has recovered from the initial shock of the idea, seems to make very good sense. Put very simply it implies a compulsion to escape from the turmoil of the world with its strident noises and its harsh lights, and to go back into the dark, quiet mystery from which we came. This desire has sometimes been compared with the Death Wish, but the analogy, I think, is false. It is not a wish for death, but for innocence, and rebirth, and above all, for peace.

True or false, the Return-to-the-Womb complex is probably present, in varying degrees, in all of us. Carried to its logical conclusion it leads to lunacy. During the last tragic months of his life Nijinsky spent day after day curled up on his bed in the shape of a foetus, with the cold Swiss sunlight shining down on an ageing body—the same body that had once enraptured the world as it danced to the silver flutes of Debussy's faun.

But this shadow should not have fallen across our page. I think that it can be sent scurrying with a smile, and a story. When a certain darling of the intelligentsia first had the complex explained to him he nodded, and flicked the ash from his cigarette. And then he said:

'I am sure that all this is true because I have the same desire myself. But . . . it *must* be a Womb with a View.'

E stands for Education.

To say that cats cannot be educated would be untrue; they are creatures of high intelligence and sensibility whose native reactions can be trained and directed. But they certainly cannot be drilled or regimented.

Dogs—yes. One can well imagine a platoon of poodles marching stiffly up and down the barrack square, and liking it. One can see them wheeling and doubling, sloping arms and presenting tails, in strict obedience to the hoarse barks of their sergeant-major. Cats, never.

(Now one comes to think of it, is it not significant that sergeant-majors of fiction invariably *bark*? They never mew. A sergeant-major who mewed—though personally I should dote on such a phenomenon—would seldom be recommended for a commission.)

This intransigence, this refusal to 'come to heel', in any sense of that unpleasantly despotic phrase, is one of the reasons why the true F finds such delight in feline companionship. He is aware that if a cat seeks him out it does so of its own free will, not because it is obeying a shouted command or pricking up its ears at a blow on the whistle. All the same, in the interests of domestic harmony, there are times when a little gentle discipline may be desirable. Hence our invention of the dinner gong.

We do not, of course, use a real gong, we merely tap a plate for the evening meal. There is no need to do this at breakfast time; every morning at seven o'clock there is a great waving of tails, lifting of paws, a brisk mewing and purring under the kitchen sink. But at tea-time it is different; the cats may be asleep, or working in the garden, or engaged on tours of inspection, or some form of espionage. So we use the 'gong' to summon them.

This is the drill. At half past four, precisely, Gaskin lays down his copy of the evening paper, emerges from his sitting-room, and goes into the tool-shed, where a saucepan containing three whiting is reposing on top of an old gas stove. (This may sound obscure. What is an old gas stove doing in the tool-shed? Your guess is as good as mine. All I know is that it is there, and that it is quite safe, because there is no gas in it.)

Then the whiting are put on three plates and carried to their appointed positions . . . Oscar's in a corner under the sink, 'Four's' by the refrigerator, and 'Five's' on the kitchen table. (Under 'Heat' I explain the deep psychological reasons which have impelled 'Five' to dine in this elevated position.)

All is now set. Gaskin takes another plate and taps it sharply and expertly—*con brio* would be the musical direction—with a fork.

Whereupon, several things happen. The first is a resounding 'plonk' from upstairs, as Oscar leaps off my bed. (Oscar is always the first to 'enter the dining-room', which is only natural, because he is the largest, the youngest, and the most energetic.) The plonk is followed by a tumble of paws down the stairs. A moment later, Oscar is dining. Next, there will be the gentle rattle of the cat-door, which signifies the entrance of 'Four'. He has almost certainly come from his watch-tower on the top of the tool-shed. As the eldest and most responsible of the cats, he selected this post from the first day of our arrival in the cottage. From here he has a wide view over all the neighbouring territory. He can keep a constant vigil on any suspicious movements by Rudolf and Webster—the cats next door. He can also keep an eye on the gardener, warn the birds off the crocuses under the copper beech, and, when autumn comes, restrain the activities of the grey squirrels who come for the nuts on the old walnut tree. If it were not for 'Four', sitting in his watch-tower, lashing his tail, I should never have a walnut at all.

The last to answer the summons of the gong is 'Five'. Although he is the plumpest, he seems to have the smallest appetite. He walks in slowly and rather haughtily, like an elderly gentleman in an expensive residential hotel making his way to his favourite corner. One feels that there should be a copy of *The Times* under his arm, and half a bottle of Médoc waiting for him, and a tin of Bath Oliver biscuits. Even when he jumps on the table he retains a certain 'hauteur'. Unlike Oscar he does not tuck in immediately; he yawns, glances round the room, sniffs, and then gives the whiting a languid dab before beginning, very daintily, to dispose of it.

This section seems to have been devoted more to Eating than to Education, but we hope that the reader will not take this amiss, in view of the fact that most of us learn the first elements of civilized behaviour at the dinner table.

As it is with eating, so it is with all the other aspects of feline education. We do not command cats, we coax them; we do not issue orders to them, we make suggestions. Sometimes, we even appeal to their sense of pity, as in the case of Oscar and the chairs. The only really effective way of stopping Oscar from ripping the upholstery is to emit a wail of anguish as soon as he begins, as though one's very flesh were being rent. And since Oscar has a fondness for one, and is quick to interpret human moods, he nearly always desists, and walks across, with a look of deep concern on his face, and rubs against one's legs to express his contrition.

But by and large, the cats remain untamed—wild creatures in a domestic setting, lions of the hearthrug, at nobody's beck and call. And this, surely, is in accordance with the conception of nature. For though man likes to think of himself as a lord of creation, this is a title which he can never earn. He may picture himself as towering above the humbler inhabitants of the universe, with undisputed dominion over fur and feather and fin, but in reality he has not the smallest dominion over any living creature. There is only one way in which he can prove his 'superiority', and that is by inflicting the death sentence. He cannot even alter the course of an ant, except by stamping on it.

To me, this is consoling. Man, in his relations with the animals, is only too apt to get above himself—to 'get on his high horse' in more senses than one. It is good that he should occasionally be reminded of his impotence, in all except this matter of inflicting the death sentence. He can shoot a pheasant, but not by a hair's breadth can he deflect the lovely design that is traced by a seagull's wings as it sweeps between the sky and the drifting spray. He can harpoon a whale; he can employ all the devices of the internal combustion engine as he flashes past in his speed-boat, tugging at some creature that he has dragged from the depths. But he cannot call the humblest minnow to his command.

And never—but never—can he control a cat.

F stands for Flowers.

Cats and flowers have played so large a part in my life that I can scarcely think of one without the other. In a cluster of wild hyacinths I can see reflected the blue eyes of my first Siamese; on warm May mornings he would wander to the shadow of an old wall where the hyacinths had come by chance, and dispose himself most elegantly upon them. If reproached for squashing the hyacinths, he merely blinked; the blue eyes and the blue flowers, mingling together, were so beautiful that there was nothing to be done about it.

Let us take a walk in the garden, to pick a bunch of flowers and bring it indoors and arrange it on a table by the piano, observing, meanwhile, how greatly we are assisted in our task by 'Four', 'Five', and Oscar.

But first, that word 'arrange' has started a train of thought which reminds me that there is something I must get off my chest, though it has no direct connection with cats. It concerns the art of flower-decoration.

This has become such a racket that nowadays if one were to do anything so simple as to pick a bunch of daffodils and drop them at random into a jam jar—which is probably how van Gogh would have chosen to paint them—one would be regarded as a Philistine. Or if, like Fantin-Latour, one disposed a few sprays of white roses in a silver bowl, and let them take their hazard of casual beauty against the breeze of an open window, one would be called to account for not sticking them in a pin-holder. Today, one must create 'significant form'. (I wonder if the women who natter about flower arrangements ever studied the works of Roger Fry?) One must have a 'musical line' or some such nonsense, and the eye must be 'brought to a central point', and the 'colour masses' must be properly balanced, etc etc.

I am criticizing, of course, the professional flower decorators, those well-meaning ladies who are for ever writing and lecturing and rushing all over the place telling their defenceless sisters what to do and how to do it. There are thousands of women who—left to their own devices—produce exquisite arrangements without ever having heard of 'vertical lines' balanced by 'harmonious triangles' or any such balderdash. My mother was one of them. She could take a spray of bramble and a few brown kitchen-garden chrysanthemums and set them in a pewter mug, and the result was magical.

But the professionals! There are a few blessed exceptions, but one wishes that most of them would go and do it at the greengrocer's, and leave the flowers alone. Consider the tortures to which they subject that poor little bunch of daffodils. Firstly, in a desperate attempt to be 'original'—how dare anybody be 'original' with a daffodil?—they group their horrid messes round a china figure. Probably a nasty little lamb from Copenhagen with a catkin stuck into its behind. They they proceed to chop off the stalks of the daffodils, to varying lengths, to get their precious 'significant form'. Finally—this is the crowning blasphemy—they so dispose the daffodils that half of them are lying in a horizontal position, as though they had been battered by a violent rain-storm.

After which they transport their 'creations' to the local flower show where doubtless they will be awarded a prize by one of their buddies.

I must check this outburst, but it had to come. I have always thought that there is only one sin—cruelty. These women are guilty of cruelty to flowers.

We may now return, faintly flushed, to the garden—and the cats.

This is the drill.

I am half way down the herbaceous border, with the first flowers gathered into the trug basket over my arm. When I began picking, at the far end, under the copper beech, the idea was to make a white bunch, which explains the cluster of white campanulas and the creamy sprays of deutzia. But then, as I stepped into the sunlight, there was a tendril of pale yellow clematis on the wall, which would look very pretty trailing over the edge of the vase. (If only one could get it to trail the right way round! Clematis is a maddening flower to arrange; it always seems to want to stand on its head.) So now the whole plan is changed. It must be a white and yellow bunch; we must go and look for some more yellows.

So here we are deep in thought, making lovely designs and colour schemes, and in all probability behaving as tiresomely as the aforesaid despised lady-decorators.

And then there is a faint tug at the basket. I look round, like a fisherman surprised by a bite. I observe that a piece of bass is trailing from the basket on to the lawn, and at the end of the bass, pouncing, is 'Five'.

At this point a faint sigh is permitted. For 'Five's' gesture cannot go unrewarded; the basket must be put down, the bass must be twitched and jerked and wiggled about, and one must run across the lawn trailing the bass, at least once, with 'Five' in hot pursuit. But all this is fatiguing and one wants to get on with the flowers and one wishes that 'Five' had chosen another time for dalliance.

However, there is an effective way of dealing with these situations, which I will pass on to fellow Fs. Two years ago, in a similar dilemma, I happened to remember that 'Five' liked sitting in baskets, particularly if they were far too small for him. So I removed the flowers, and put them in a bucket under the copper beech. Then, returning to 'Five', I pushed him over on his back, scooped him up, and inserted him sideways into the trug basket, pushing him down under the handle and moulding him in, as though one were kneading a loaf. These attentions, to my relief, were well received, and when I lifted up the basket, he stayed in it quite placidly, purring, with his tail hanging over the edge. We were both pleased with ourselves; 'Five' was diverted by this new method of transport, which gave him an opportunity of seeing the lupins at eye-level; and I had all the agreeable sensations of taking baby out in the pram.

So now, when I go out to gather a mixed bunch, there are always two baskets. One for the flowers and one for 'Five'.

I am sure that cats love flowers, or at least, that there is some sort of mystic attraction between them. It cannot be by pure chance that a Siamese always seeks out blue flowers, to go with his eyes. We have already met my beloved 'One', a king among cats, as he lay by the wild hyacinths. But he also chose to dispose himself among clumps of delphiniums and love-in-the-mist. Always blue.

The primary attraction, presumably, is one of scent. Here cats are more drawn to the kitchen-garden. They seem to be unmoved by the perfume of roses or magnolias or such-like, but they do a great deal of very pretty and intense sniffing round a bed of lovage or tarragon or apple mint. And, of course, valerian.

The mention of valerian brings me in reluctant opposition to that formidable old gentleman Mr W. Robinson. In his classic volume

The English Flower Garden, he is contemptuous of this amiable and nostalgic plant. I call it 'amiable' because it will grow in a handful of dust on a windswept wall. And nostalgic because it brings to mind many summer hours of childhood, when it brushed my cheeks as I climbed the cliffs of Land's End, to the challenge of the smooth, dark seas below, and the cry of the seagulls all around.

Mr Robinson considers that the valerian is a 'common' plant and he proclaims, on page 678 of the sixteenth edition of his otherwise admirable book, that the flowers are 'unpleasantly scented'. This statement lays Mr Robinson open to grave suspicions of being non-F. For how could a flower be 'common' or 'unpleasantly scented' when its odour, throughout the summer months, attracts a long train of royal—if somewhat scruffy—personages, who stalk proudly up to it, sniff it, and then, turning their backs ... But let this picture dissolve, as it were, in a cloud of perfumed prose.

And let us ring down the curtain on a quiet garden, during a sultry afternoon in July, with the cats disposed in their accustomed positions. Oscar, stretched out among the rushes by the pond, occasion-

ally extending a languid paw over the water, as a fish darts by with a flash of silver. 'Four', a limp, languid lump of fur, curled up on the parched earth in the shadow of the old white rose tree, that occasionally lets a snowy petal flutter down on to to his back, so that he twitches and opens a green eye, and then goes to sleep again.

And 'Five', gravely stalking me as I go out to pick the flowers, with the bass trailing behind. And being lifted up, and moulded into the spare basket, and being carried round in a stately promenade.

So now you will realize why, when I look into a bunch of flowers, I always seem to see the gleam of cats' eyes through the blossom.

G stands for graves and Epitaphs.

A gloomy subject? That depends on your view of life—and of death.

One of the happiest and most tranquil places I ever visited was the animals' sanctuary in Tangier. I had motored out there in a truck belonging to the People's Dispensary for Sick Animals. I was in need of solace. The Arabs are not renowned for their kindness to animals;[1] they are not deliberately cruel, but they seem incapable of realizing that animals can suffer at all or—even if they do realize it—that it is any concern of theirs. This was why I was thankful to escape for a while from the dark, winding alleys of Tangier, where skeletal dogs slunk shivering into the darkness, and starving cats fought for scraps of dusty skin and bone under the barrows in the fish market.

The sanctuary was five miles from the city, on the way to the bare, saffron-coloured hills. It lay off the main road in a gentle curving valley, through which there ran a stream on whose banks a group of women were drying the weekly wash. It was a cool, clear day of brilliant sunshine; there was a hint of spring in the air; the fields

[1] Thanks to the P.D.S.A. there has been a marked improvement since my visit.

were starred with white narcissi and under the bare trees there were pools of white violets. I remember thinking how gay and pleasant a picture it all made—the white sheets the women were washing, the white flowers in the meadows, all under the cold, clean, blue sky.

We turned off the rutted track and took the path to the cemetery, neatly disposed in a near-by field, with wild almonds blooming around. About a hundred animals were buried there, mostly cats and dogs that had been brought over from England to end their days by the side of their masters and mistresses. A few of the graves were overgrown, but most of them were tidy and well-tended, and on several there were fresh flowers, violets, and narcissi from the local fields, sprays of mimosa from the hedgerows on the hill. Each grave had a name engraved on it, and often there were simple mottoes and tags of verse which I will not quote; out of their context they might sound foolish.

But that was not how they seemed to me, standing there under the young almond trees with nothing but the tinkling of the stream to break the silence. Inevitably—and doubtless with blatant sentimentality—I recall Rupert Brooke. 'If I should die, think only this of me: That there's some corner of a foreign field That is for ever England. There shall be In that rich earth a richer dust concealed . . .'

No, a very humble dust, mingling with the alien soil of Africa. This dust was all that was left of many greatly loved little creatures, dogs who had snuffled through the bracken of English moors, cats who had scampered over the lawns of English gardens—little creatures who had given many hours of delight and laughter to their masters and mistresses—and in their passing, had left a great sadness. Was it so foolish, so sentimental, that the delight should be honoured and the grief commemorated?

Maybe I am the wrong person to write these words. Concerning the disposition of my own remains, 'I couldn't care less'—a vulgar phrase, but apposite. If one believes in the survival of the spirit, what happens to the body is surely of the smallest importance? They can do anything they like with my own. As long as—to quote the immortal remark of Mrs Patrick Campbell, when she was discussing certain forms of illicit love-making—'as long as they don't do it in the street and frighten the horses'.

But somehow, with animals it is different. Perhaps this is because they were cast in such humble roles while they were alive that when they are dead we feel the need of making a belated gesture to acknowledge their importance. For after all, the very fact that they *have* died makes them important; they are a step further on the road; they have seen through the curtain, even if the eyes are those of a dead kitten, lying in the gutter. They have achieved this importance, as Thomas Hardy wrote, 'by crossing at a breath, into safe and shielded death'. And merely because they have 'taken hence their insignificance' they

> Loom as largened to the sense,
> Shape as part, above man's will,
> Of the Imperturbable.

This same thought moved an American poet when she wrote:

> What was warm is strangely cold—
> When dissolved the little breath?
> How could this small body hold
> So immense a thing as Death?[1]

That is why a grave for an animal is neither ridiculous nor illogical, and why this little sanctuary at Tangier was one of the most moving places I have ever visited.

When we left I strolled up into the hills to pick mimosa—an activity which has a special thrill of its own. To be able to gather up armfuls of this golden blossom, without paying for it, gives one something of the sensation of robbing a bank. Then I sat down and looked back over the valley towards the sanctuary and thought how nice it would be to be buried in it oneself. Perhaps one could reserve a small plot? I had noticed a blank space under one of the almond trees, between two Scotch pussies, who had lived to a great age, and a Devonshire bulldog. They would be pleasant companions in the

[1] 'For a Dead Kitten'—Sara Hay

Elysian fields. Yes, it would be a very nice place indeed, but I doubted whether it could be arranged. Somebody would be sure to object; and it is quite possible there would be something against it in the Prayer Book. Besides, I did not really crave even so meek a sepulchre—not for myself.

But for 'Four' and 'Five' and Oscar it would be different. Indeed, as I sat on the hillside staring across the valley, with the golden blossoming treasure resting on my knee, I found myself devising the most superior mausoleums to suit their various personalities. 'Four's' would be of jet, with a frieze of golden claws. 'Five's' would be faintly feminine and decidedly rococo, and the walls would be encrusted with festoons of peridots. Oscar's would be very striking, with a vaulted ceiling decorated by the fins of fishes, executed in jade.

A plague on these premature forebodings! At the moment of writing, all the cats are so brimful of health and spirits that I strongly suspect—and hope—that they will be the principal participants in my own cortège. That will indeed give them a glorious opportunity to exhibit their special talents. 'Four', the Cat Who Does the Act, will never have had a more moving role. I can see him, as I have often seen him, jet black, head sunk in grief, tail trailing to the mournful lilt of Chopin's funeral march. (One hopes that he will have

some sort of audience, apart from Gaskin and the daily woman.) Oscar, I know, will bear himself like a man, though I hope that he does not make any of his heartbreaking little snuffling noises, which he makes when he is sad, because I should be unable to get out of the coffin and comfort him.

And 'Five'? He will be at the back, paws moving strictly in rhythm, tail erect, whiskers shining. But his ears will be at the alert. For this would be an occasion where 'The Iceman Cometh'. Icemen, presumably, have much in common with dustmen. And we all know what 'Five' thinks about *them*.

H stands for Heat.

Once, during the war, in the depths of a bitter winter, I journeyed north to stay with the late Sir Compton Mackenzie on his island in the Hebrides, for some obscure reason which I have now forgotten.

And there, sitting on top of a hot stove in the kitchen, were four elderly Siamese cats.

It was a most impressive moment in one's life.

Outside, the winds howled and raged through the stunted pines. Icy spray lashed the windows and the paths were strewn with tattered sea-weed. The witches of *Macbeth* would have been in their element, and the whole occasion was made the more melodramatic by the fact that the whole island was alive with illicit lights. The inhabitants, with a fine Scottish independence and a lofty disregard for 'enemy action'—how dated that nasty phrase sounds today!—paid small heed to the black-out which was smothering the South. With the result that through the scream of the wind and the hiss of the rain I fancied that I heard the menacing growl of hostile aircraft.

Against this lurid background the elderly Siamese cats sat on the burning stove, gazing with veiled blue eyes into the distance, thinking lofty Siamese thoughts. They reminded me of four Eastern ladies of the utmost distinction giving their fatigued attention to some ceremonial occasion. The only thing that worried me about this touching episode was that their sit-upons might be scorched.

I approached the stove, held out my arms to the eldest and most imperial of the cats, and, after making the proper obeisances, was successful in persuading it to be gently elevated. (This round-about phrase may perhaps only be understood by advanced Fs. A non-F would write 'I picked it up.' I did no such thing, I repeat—'I was successful in persuading it to be gently elevated.' If this distinction is not crystal clear, you must put down this work and take the corgi for a walk.)

And I discovered that the Siamese's sit-upon was, indeed, scorching. I will not go so far as to say that I could not bear my hand on it, but if one's own sit-upon had been half as hot one would have been in great distress. Yet, here was this sensitive creature, quite unmoved. Mentally baptizing her Honourable Lady Hot-Situpon of the Northern Isles I rearranged her on the top of the stove. You will not be surprised to learn that the moment her sit-upon touched the stove, she began to purr, like a kettle when you put it back on the gas ring.

The whole subject of cats and heat is absorbing, not only biologically but psychologically. The devices they employ in their efforts to keep warm shed a revealing light on their characters.

Consider 'Four'—the Cat Who Does the Act. He invariably takes advantage of any cold spell to put on a virtuoso exhibition of being maltreated. Although he has a comfortable armchair next to the radiator in Gaskin's room—or for that matter, a corner of several warm beds and plenty of room in the linen cupboard—he scorns such obvious resorts. They afford no scope for his talents.

So what happens? 'Four', heaving tragic sighs, and casting agonized looks over his shoulder, stalks heavily to the fire-place in the music-room. And then—poor forsaken creature—he curls up beside the dying ash, and disposes himself to sleep. Time and again I have gone up to him and said ' "Four", you are being too ridiculous. The wood-ash will be cold by the morning. What is more, it will get on your tail, and when you lick it off, it will get into your system. And though wood-ash is very good for lupins I cannot believe that it is good for elderly black cats. Apart from that, when you creep out in the morning, you will leave a trail of wood-ash all over the carpet, which will not be popular with Gaskin.'

But 'Four' pays no heed. He is far too engrossed in his role. So I shake my head, and bid him good-night, hoping that there will be no late callers to observe him crouched by the embers. Sure enough, in the morning he is still there, forlorn and hunched up, with a large blob of wood-ash on the end of his nose, when all he need do to get warm is walk a few yards to a blazing fire in the next room. There are no limits to the sacrifices which 'Four' will make in the exercise of his art.

'Five's' behaviour is equally revealing. 'Five', in spite of his deceptive *embonpoint*, is a bundle of nerves, owing to the unfortunate episode in his youth when he leapt out of an upstairs window while fleeing from a Pekinese. 'Five' is always the first to sound the tocsin on Tuesday mornings, when the dustmen come, rushing into the house from the garden with wild eyes and a bristling tail, as though the devil were at his heels. His choice of sleeping quarters, too, is always governed by strategic considerations; he likes to repose himself where nobody can come upon him unawares. For this reason

his favourite spot is on a shelf at the top of the staircase, where he can lie, as in a watch-tower, with one green eye half open, on the look-out for any suspicious characters such as the grocer's boy.

And so, when winter strikes, when there is ice on the pond and the lawn is as hard as rock, and when I wrap up every morning in order to offer moral support to the delicate little eucalyptus trees in the far corner—for this is the only form of comfort I can give them and I believe it works—'Five' hies himself to the dark recesses of the linen cupboard. He walks upstairs slowly and sedately, with tail erect, sits outside the door, and emits a faint mew, which means, 'This is linen-cupboard weather. Kindly let me in.' So we open the door, and he leaps up, progressing from shelf to shelf, till he reaches the top, where he curls up on an old patchwork and indicates, by a yawn,

that he is quite comfortable and that one may take one's leave. He is warm, he is at ease, best of all, he is safe; even the dustmen would never think of looking for him here.

And Oscar? By now, you are probably enough in Oscar's confidence to guess that he does not greatly care how he keeps warm as long as he is in company. He would rather lie on a luke-warm lap than stretch himself before the brightest fire in an empty room. The front door has only to open, on a snowy night, and he will jump up from the sybaritic heat of the radiator, and start his welcome of weaving and curling before one has time to take off one's overcoat. Of all the cats I have ever known, Oscar is the most constant in his demand for human companionship; he is the classic answer to all those foolish slanders about feline cupboard love which are current in more barbaric outposts of the non-F world.

Which will be enough about Heat. Graver problems await us, so let us leave our little trio in their chosen places—'Four' exhibiting his histrionic skill against the wood-ash, 'Five', betraying his complexes in the linen cupboard, and Oscar, curled up on a corner of my desk, making playful dabs at my pen. Which, I hope, may serve as an excuse for any occasional crudities in the composition of this opus.

J

Insomnia.

Cats are the best cure for insomnia that has yet been invented. In every well-appointed clinic for nervous diseases there should be a large Feline Annex, stocked with quantities of plump and amiable pussies, ready to be scooped up by expert attendants, carried down well-warmed corridors, and gently deposited on the unquiet beds of the insomniacs. The rest would be silence. Or even better than silence—gentle sighs and quiet purrs.

Specially privileged patients, or those in the more acute stages, might be permitted to sleep in the Annex itself, on large, soft couches where they would receive the combined soporific attentions of several pussies at the same time. I have often thought that this would be the acme of sensuous delight, to be wafted to repose in an enormous living bundle of sleepy, purring fur.

Of my three cats the most potent, as a 'knocker-outer', is 'Four'. By 'knocker-outer' I mean something like the red tablets one's doctor prescribes when the green ones are not strong enough. I am not a drug addict, and a single green one, taken about once a month, is enough for the normal routine. Sometimes, however, there is a crisis, and a nervous danger signal. Then I go to the medicine cupboard and take out the little bottle with the red tablets. But in nine cases out of ten I put it back again unopened, because I have remembered 'Four'. Why resort to expensive drugs when one can employ, free of charge, the services of inexpensive felines?

So I tiptoe downstairs, usually at about one a.m., and open the door of Gaskin's sitting-room, which is the room where 'Four' and 'Five' sleep when the weather is not cold enough for 'Four' to do his act or for 'Five' to seek the linen-cupboard.

There is 'Four', a small, densely black bundle, in the red armchair under the photograph of Edith Evans in *Evensong*. There too is 'Five', in the blue armchair under the photograph of himself sitting on the balustrade in the garden of 'Merry Hall'. Both cats open their eyes, and blink in the sudden light. Both immediately grasp the situation. 'Five' sends a sidelong glance to 'Four', which means 'This is where you have to do your stuff'. 'Four' gives a prodigious yawn, to indicate that he is drenched in an aura of sleep, which he is prepared to share with me.

Whereupon he rises, arches his back, stretches out his front paws, yawns again, shakes himself, and observes: 'I am at your disposal. You may carry me upstairs.'

Which I do. Even as he snuggles in my arms, negotiating the dark staircase, I have a feeling of relaxation. When I push open the door of my bedroom with my elbow the room seems strangely hushed. A few minutes ago the sounds drifting through the open window had been restless and disturbing; there had been an uneasy creak in the branches of the walnut tree and a tiresome rattle from the window blind. The screech owls had been unpleasantly close. But now the owls have flown away, and the wind has dropped, and the walnut tree has ceased its mutterings and is sighing itself to rest.

And so is 'Four'. As I deposit him on the bed, in the same scooped-up position, intact, he has forgotten all his nonsense about being the Maltreated Cat. He sets to work, quietly and efficiently, to bring peace to his restless master.

First, he adjusts the pillows. They must be a little higher, in order that he may curl into the crook of my arm without being squashed. Then he slightly rearranges the blankets. They must not be pulled too close or they will cause his ears to twitch, and that would disturb the therapeutical processes. After which he usually gives a faint sneeze, as a signal that the lights may now be turned out.

So we are in darkness. And 'Four' is very warm, and from his small body a strange, soothing balm is stealing. This is accompanied by the gentlest, finger-tip movement of the paws, and ... of course ... a slow, steady purr. The purr is regulated with the utmost art. If I stroke him, he takes this as a signal that I am not yet quite prepared for Morpheus, and the purr ascends a few notes in the scale, and is given a faint *vibrato*, suggestive of the cooing of doves. But if my hand rests beside him, slack and inert, the purr is soft-pedalled, and dies away to the faintest of sighs, which blend with the dying whispers of the wind, till all is lost in a blessed silence.

How far we have to travel before we even begin to understand the essentials of civilized comfort! One can stay at the grandest hotels, where the bedrooms are soft and sumptuous, and where the bathrooms are glittering jewel-boxes of oriental luxury. By the side of

one's bed is a little contraption with buttons that ring bells to summon every sort of slave—a slave to take one's laundry, to bring a jug of ice-water, to provide an elaborate meal, to cut one's hair, to pull up the blinds, to turn down the counterpane. But there is no bell marked F, to put one in touch with the Feline Services Department. One day I should like to establish such an hotel.

However, there would be a slight but significant difference. It would be the cats who would lie in bed, pressing the bells, and the humans who would answer them.

J stands for Jealousy.

Our drama is set on a sunny morning in the shadow of the walnut tree, and it begins with a very faint sound which you would probably not notice unless you were waiting for it—the soft whisper of fragments of walnut shell fluttering through the branches.

Down they fall, with a gentle pitter-patter, and they land at the feet of 'Five', who loftily ignores them. Rather, he pretends to ignore them, for he is sitting very still, presuming himself to be unobserved by the squirrel above. The presumption, of course, is absurd. The squirrel is fully aware of 'Five's' presence. And I am certain that he is aiming the fragments of shell directly at 'Five's' head, in a spirit of squirrelish bravado.

A swift twitch of 'Five's' tail informs me that he is beginning to be bored. One cannot sit for hours under walnut trees, being mocked, without some promise of action, and no action is pending. The squirrel, high up in the topmost branches, is surrounded by a positive bevy of walnuts; he could stay there all the morning, nibbling and spitting out those small, insulting particles. So 'Five'

decides to call it a day. He yawns, stretches, and stalks forward to the trunk of the tree, on which he proceeds to sharpen his claws. He sharpens them thoroughly and methodically, with an occasional glance upwards, as though to warn the squirrel of what to expect if he continues in his outrageous conduct.

Then 'Five' turns, notices me, and promptly falls flat on his back.

As an experienced F, I correctly interpret this gesture as a sign that tummy-rubbing is demanded. 'Five's' posture is in the classic tradition; the front paws are dangling, the hind legs are slightly apart, the head is tilted to one side, there is a come-hither glint in the green eyes. The whole position has a coyness which does not quite accord with 'Five's' *embonpoint*. But its meaning is unmistakable. Tummy-rubbing is the order of the moment. Needless to say, I obey the order.

I walk across, like an obedient slave, and set to work, supplying a variant with the under-the-chin stroke, and an occasional sharp, well-timed tweak of the tail. This demands a high standard of technique and should never be attempted except by advanced students. After a few minutes I pause, for the morning is very hot, and it is tiring work bending down.

And then, to my dismay, I notice a small black shape crouched in the door of the tool-shed. Hist . . . we are observed! 'Four', having been informed by some mystic sense that tummy-rubbing is in the air, has crept out to watch, and is regarding us with despair, grief, hatred, and a general sense of total desolation. How a small, black shape in the shadows, illuminated by only two green eyes, can convey such a complex of powerful emotions, I do not pretend to understand. But he does.

And talking of cats' eyes, is it not significant that cats are the only animals who look Man straight in the face, who are undeterred by the most arrogant human stare? If you stare at a dog the poor creature will be embarrassed, fidgeting and averting its eyes. If it were capable of blushing, it would blush. Even puppies, however gently you may speak to them, do not care for prolonged scrutiny; their reactions are much the same as those of schoolboys with a guilty conscience; it is almost as though they were plagued by a sense of original sin. If you stare at a parrot it will stare back for a little while but it is obviously none too happy about the situation, and begins to fiddle about on its perch, and turn its back and scratch its head. If you stare at a monkey its reactions are much the same as a human's. They betray embarrassment, and occasionally, particularly if they are incarcerated in a zoo, rage—which is, of course, a manifestation of fear. But cats return your gaze candidly, with no sign of perturbation. They do not blink, they do not lower their sights, the cool green eyes remain fixed on yours, making their calm appraisal. Perhaps this natural phenomenon is responsible for the phrase 'A cat may look at a queen'. In any staring match the queen would certainly be outmatched.

However, we were on the threshold of tragedy, with 'Four' in the wings, demanding instant attention. So I give a final expert stroke to 'Five's' chin and hurry over to the tool-shed. The reaction is as I expected. 'Four' immediately starts the Act. Terror is registered, and he darts away. I follow, making soothing noises. He retreats further, and then pauses looking back at me, with his head over his shoulder. If I were sensible—or if 'Four' were a dog—I should also pause, fold my arms, and say to him 'Very well, "Four", if you persist in this idiotic behaviour, that is your own affair. But if you wish to be stroked, like a good cat, you will kindly come over here and assume a stroking posture.' But I am not sensible, and 'Four' is not a dog, so I make a sudden dart, and seize him, and begin the stroking.

The technique demanded by 'Four' differs *in toto* from the technique demanded by 'Five'. The stroking must be far more robust, beginning at the back of the neck, ending at the base of the tail, and marked by a strong *vibrato*. As it increases in vigour it must be accompanied by sharp taps on the spine. If non-Fs were to observe this performance they would be confirmed in their conviction that I *am* a cat-beater, particularly as 'Four' shows his approval of them by a very peculiar blend of purrs and mews. (The reader will have guessed that 'Four', mentally and physically, has a strong streak of masochism.) However, they would be puzzled by the fact that when I stop, 'Four' makes no effort to escape, but remains there demanding more, with his behind elevated at an angle of forty-five degrees.

The stroking continues. And then, suddenly, a shadow falls on this strange scene—the shadow of a tail held very erect, coming towards us, like an accusing finger. Once again, we have been observed! I do not have to turn in order to see whose tail it is. Nor does Oscar turn as he passes, for he would not deign to cast a glance on such sickening proceedings. Scorn is written all over him . . . it is in his walk, in his whiskers, in his tail, even in his behind.

I know what he is saying to me. '"Four" has had more than his share of back-stroking. "Five" has had more than his share of tummy-rubbing. Unless a little attention is given to *me*, there will be hell to pay.'

I know too where he is going, because the drill is always the same. He is making for the old pear tree. As soon as he reaches it, he will sniff the trunk. Then, with a single Nijinsky leap, scarcely touching the bark, he will land in the fork of the first branch, about six feet above the ground. Whereupon he will dispose himself for dalliance, with his right paw dangling languidly in front of him, ready to pounce on any prey that may present itself.

The dalliance, of course, has to be supplied by myself, and supplied quickly. So 'Four' gets a final stroke—long and lingering, to give him the idea that I am parting from him only with the greatest reluctance. And I walk across the lawn to report for duty at the pear tree.

Which shall it be? A twig? A blade of grass? An iris leaf? (I need hardly explain to Fs that I am pondering on the best form of decoy to dangle before Oscar's claws—to sweep up and down the trunk for him to pounce upon.) I pause before a cluster of lupins that have gone to seed. A lupin stick might do. The pods make an exciting rattle. But they are inclined to break off if the pounce is too energetic, leaving me only with the stump, and it is difficult to get real drama into the dalliance if one only has a stump. (An observation which, when one comes to think of it, might come more fittingly from the lips of a Manx.) Twigs, too, break off too easily, and sometimes get stuck in Oscar's teeth. It had better be the iris leaf. So I pick a nice long one—the clump is getting seriously denuded—advance to the tree, and set to work.

Up and down sweeps the iris leaf, always just out of reach of Oscar's paws. It is a moment of intense and exhausting concentration, because when you are playing this game you must project yourself into the leaf; it must be part of your own body; you must be fleeing in peril of your life. Sometimes he nearly catches me, but I am too cunning for him, I switch—via the leaf—into a crook in the pear tree, trembling, alert, and then dart up again. Oscar's tail lashes, his green eyes glisten, his sharp claws pounce and pounce again. At last, out of sheer fatigue, I let myself be caught. For a moment Oscar pretends to devour me, and then he lets the leaf fall to the ground. The dalliance is concluded. I am allowed to take my departure.

So I walk slowly back to the house, watched by three pairs of eyes. 'Four' on the lawn, 'Five' under the walnut, Oscar in the pear tree. Very different eyes, that mirror very different personalities. But those eyes have one thing in common. They are all green.

K stands for Kittens.

It will be generally agreed that babies, when compared with kittens, are very unattractive creatures.

The chief objection to babies is that they are insane. I came into the world as a lunatic and so did you, and only through a long and painful process of education did we develop into 'civilized' men and women—which means, of course, another form of lunatic, though not such a comparatively harmless one.

If we were deposited as babies on a desert island we should remain the gibbering idiots that we were at birth. Having no knowledge of any alphabet we should be unable to communicate our thoughts; indeed, we should have no thoughts to communicate; we should be guided only by the most primitive instincts. And even in these instincts we would show ourselves greatly inferior to kittens. Consider such an elementary matter as sanitation. Monkeys, the closest relatives to man in the animal kingdom, have no instinct for sanitation at all, as may be observed by paying the most cursory visit to the zoo. Our deserted babies would be equally devoid of such instincts. The smallest and wildest kitten, however, would behave impeccably; it would powder its nose and wash its hands as though it were descended from a long line of ancestors who had been accustomed to a high standard of plumbing since the days of Neanderthal man.

The doting mother, as she bends over the cradle, crooning to its bald and maniac occupant, may possibly question these observations. If she does, she can scarcely escape the charge of being non-F. Better for her to accept the truth, tuck up baby for the night, and go out to sit by the kitten basket, in order to study the behaviour of civilized young creatures.

The advent of a new kitten, in a really F household, is, or should be, a major event in the lives of all concerned. For several years a new kitten has, as it were, been hovering on my horizon, but nothing has come of it. My favourite clairvoyant, Mr Corbett, has definitely seen a kitten in his crystal ball, but he cannot forecast the date of its arrival. It is there, somewhere, in the clouds, but evidently suitable conjunction of the planets has not as yet occurred. Sometimes I suspect that this is due to the psychic influence of 'Four' and Oscar. Whenever a new kitten is being discussed, 'Four' seizes the opportunity to give a supreme performance of his role, sighing, sitting in corners, and retreating even further into the fire-place in order to cover himself in symbolic ashes. Oscar becomes more than ever clamorous for attention, and gazes at one with such an excess of sentimentality and possessiveness that one dreads to think what would happen if he were suddenly to find a kitten on one's lap. The only person who is sensible about the whole thing is 'Five'. He has often made it clear that he would welcome some new blood in the household, and on the rare occasions when he has encountered kittens in neighbouring gardens, has given a brilliant display of kittenishness himself, in spite of his *embonpoint*.

Concerning the habits of kittens many volumes might be written ... from the time they lie suckling in the basket, pressing their small velvet paws in a gentle rhythm against their mother's breast, through those enchanted stages when they open their blues eyes which slowly turn to green, like tiny pools over which the clouds have drifted, and over the thrilling weeks in which they stagger out of the basket and gradually gain strength and grace in a series of wild adventures. There is no dull moment in all their exquisite adolescence, which would provide material for an Encyclopaedia Felinica.

In this comparatively modest work I have space for only one observation, which concerns the instinctive 'come-back' of kittens to the stimulus of danger. This is an awful subject, in the literal sense that one is filled with awe when one contemplates the miraculous delicacy of Nature's signalling system, whereby a menacing echo borne on the wind can set in motion a whole complex of glandular and muscular reactions. Blake paused, in immortal astonishment, before the 'fearful symmetry' of his Tiger. I pause—though not for posterity—in equal astonishment, before the fearful symmetry of a kitten.

Watch what happens when a kitten is confronted by any potential menace, such as an unfamiliar cat. Its immediate reaction is to make itself appear larger and more formidable. And so it abruptly switches its body sideways. At the same time it arches its back and stands on tiptoe. While it is assuming this strange posture the fur rises all over its body, puffing it out and transforming its tail into the semblance of a fox's brush. Thus caparisoned—the word seems justified, for

one has the feeling that the kitten is clad in a sort of ghostly armour—the kitten slowly advances.

This sequence of movements must surely be one of the most elaborate, as it is certainly one of the most beautiful, performed by any young creature in nature. Merely to describe it has made me realize how much I am missing, in my present kittenless condition. I must ring up Mr Corbett, and ask him to look once again into his crystal ball.

L stands for Laughter.

But not—let us be very clear about this—not what we call 'mocking laughter'. To make an animal feel ridiculous is unpardonable. This is one of the principal reasons why I loathe the circus. If a man chooses to chalk his face, paint his nose, and stand on his head, good luck to him. He may look less ludicrous in this posture than when he is strap-hanging in a bowler hat. But for God's sake let him keep his hands off the animals.

I sometimes indulge in the diversion of creating special hells for persons whom I most dislike. Among these imaginary infernos is one reserved for circus proprietors, lion-tamers, ring-masters, bull-fighters, and the like. In this arena of my dreams the audience and the animals swop places. The front stalls are filled by quantities of very beautiful lions, fanning themselves with their programmes. The dress circle is packed with an uproarious collection of dogs, of all shapes and sizes ... a good-natured crowd, but determined to get their money's worth. The boxes are reserved for the elephants. (Sometimes, when the dream is very vivid, I give the elephants tiaras.) Prowling round at the back, tossing their manes, are the horses, looking very white and wonderful, and quite free to run out into the night as soon as they are bored.

Then the show begins. And what a show it is! The whips crack round the naked calves of the lion-tamers. (All done by kindness!) The flames leap up as the ringmasters are put through the hoop. (They really *love* it, you know!) And as a grand finale, the directors of the circus company (who have been equipped for the occasion with artificial tails) are suspended from the roof, in which position they are fed with gingerbreads soaked in rancid South African sherry. All to the uproarious applause of the aforementioned lions, dogs, elephants, and horses ... to say nothing of a certain rather proletarian orang-outang in the gallery and a pair of cheeky marmosets in the pit, whose behaviour is too impolite to describe in detail, even though one may sympathize with it.

Well—I have got *that* off my chest. So now we can relax, and come from the general to the particular, and focus the spotlight on to the small pink object which inspired these observations ... Oscar's tongue.

All Fs, of course, will have delighted in those rather absurd moments, when they have glanced up from a book by the fire, or paused in their knitting, to see pussy observing them, with the end of the tongue sticking out. It looks like the tip of a rose petal stuck below the nose, and pussy appears to be quite unconscious that it is out at all. You may call attention to it ... you may say 'My dear

"Four", are you aware that your tongue is sticking out?' 'Four' does not seem to hear you. You may even remark, quite severely ... '"Five", if you keep your tongue out like that, one day the wind will change and you will never be able to put it in again.' No heed is taken. In Oscar's case, you may even bend down and stroke him, in the hope that this will induce a change of mood and a consequent withdrawal of the tongue. It does no such thing. All that happens is that when Oscar starts to purr, as always, the purr has a faintly sibilant quality, a sort of twang, which brings back a faint echo of my childhood, when I sometimes used to put sheets of music on the open wires of our old Broadwood piano, to simulate a guitar. The tongue remains out.

And it really is—let's face it—rather funny.

But I am quite sure that we should not laugh at it—not, at least, in pussy's face. The tongue-protruding is a symbol of peace and contentment and trust and affection. One does not sit for long periods on a mat with one's tongue out, gazing with swimming eyes at somebody at least ten times larger than oneself, if one is in any immediate anxiety about one's personal security.

And yet, one *wants* to laugh. The trouble, of course, is anthropomorphic; it arises from our terrible habit of translating animal habits into human terms. If, for example, we found ourselves in a box at the opera in the company of an exquisite female and if, during one of the *longueurs* of *Siegfried* we found that the delicious creature was regarding us from under her languorous lashes with a small, pointed cerise tongue protruding from her lips, we might well be excused for suspecting that some peculiar form of badinage was being suggested. In which case, we would react according to our temperaments. My own reaction would almost certainly be a swift exit to the bar.

I am not absolutely certain—for after all one is something of a pioneer in these problems—of the ultimate F ruling in this dilemma: of what, in short, the F should actually *do*—though I rather suspect, while emphasizing that I am speaking without the Book, no true and authoritative Book as yet being in existence (and I trust that the reader will forgive this parody, however momentarily, of Henry

James, whom let us salute in passing as F from tip to toe) . . . I rather suspect that the *true* F, the ideal F, the shiningly impeccable F, would put his tongue out too.

One day, I am going to try it. I shall be sitting at my desk, writing beautiful thoughts, and I shall look across the room and there by the fire will be Oscar, lying on his back, with his front paws dangling before him, gazing at me with his tongue out. And I shall lay down my pen, and put my tongue out too. And neither of us will laugh.

M stands for Milk.

I have just been watching 'Five' drink his milk. It is a curious operation, for he does not really drink it at all. He stands in front of it, and then, very languidly, produces a paw which he dips in the milk. He proceeds to lick the paw, with a faintly supercilious expression, as though he were savouring a vintage wine.

One is reminded of a French marquise dipping sponge-cakes into green Chartreuse under the chandeliers of Versailles. I doubt if there is any historical authority for suggesting that French marquises ever did anything so vulgar, even in 1788, but it is the sort of thing that one remembers from childhood readings of Carlyle and *A Tale of Two Cities*.

'Five', in spite of his mixed origin and the cockney smudge on his nose, has an aura of aristocracy. If he had lived in the eighteenth century he could have outstared any French marquise, even the Comtesse de Polignac. He is so fussy that on the flight to Varennes he would have been a considerable encumbrance; but if I had had anything to do with it, he would have been given the best seat.

(Pause for thought. Was Marie Antoinette F? My instinctive retort to this question is 'No'. I feel that she probably drifted about with rather raffish borzois who would have been the better for a good scrubbing. Though, once again, I have no historical authority for this suggestion. Danton, most certainly, was F, and so was Robespierre, though he was very wicked and scratchy, and up-to-no-good around the railings of the Palais Royal. A great deal of human misery might have been averted if Robespierre had been 'arranged'. But that, after all, might be said of most of the great 'heroes' of history, from Alexander onward.)

To return to 'Five' and his milk—for I must constantly remind myself that this is intended to be a serious work, destined for the shelves of eminent veterinary surgeons.

One of the most common delusions of the non-F world is that every cat likes milk, and that if only they have enough of it, all will be well. But all cats do *not* like milk. Consider my own little family. 'Five' as we have seen regards milk as an aperitif. 'Four' scarcely regards it at all. He prefers water—of which, needless to say, there is always a bowl under the sink. Occasionally, after eating his fish, he will stalk past the milk saucer and then pause, glance over his shoulder, and—if anybody is watching—heave a deep sigh, retrace his steps, and take a few timid sips.

But 'Four's' favourite beverage, when he is allowed it, is soda water, and I think that this must be due to the streak of Siamese in him. I originally encountered this curious taste for soda water in my Siamese cat 'One', now alas departed from this world. He was first attracted to it, obviously, by his discovery that soda water syphons frequently leaked, making strange hissing noises, and producing drops which trembled on the tips of the spouts—drops which must be attended to, and dabbed at. Many is the time that I have come into the dining-room to find 'One' dabbing at the drops, with a little pool of soda water forming beneath the syphon, spoiling the veneer. After a while I began to grow suspicious. Surely the syphons were becoming less and less efficient? Surely it was strange that so many of them should be leaking like this? And then, one day, I caught him in the act, with his paw on the handle, giving it a series of sharp dabs to make it work. After which, the syphons were placed in a less accessible position, and the table gradually regained its veneer.

'Four' has not resorted to such knavish tricks. However, he gets his soda water all the same, for he always seems to know when it is being used. He likes it at its fizziest, and he drinks it from a saucer, giving an occasional sneeze when a bubble goes up his nose.

But we were speaking of milk.

The only inveterate milk-drinker in my family is Oscar, who absorbs it like a sponge. Every morning, as soon as I have been presented with the breakfast tray, Oscar puts his head through the door, steps forward, and leaps on to the bed. He has come for his milk, but he is a stickler for etiquette and he knows that certain ceremonial procedures must first be observed before he actually demands it. First, he must give a sharp swish to my letters, sending them on to the floor. Next, he must sit on the *Daily Telegraph*, and—if possible—so disarrange it that I shall be unable to read the leader. He would not like me to be depressed by its sombre tone. Finally, he must have a little organ practice, pressing his paws up and down with great fervour on the keys (my ankles) and gazing at me, and through me, with such an intensity of musical emotion that I can almost hear the strains of the Lost Chord.

He is now ready for his milk, which I pour out in a saucer on the tray ... thinking, as I do so, how wonderful it would be, for once in a way, to be able to drink a cup of coffee with a saucer attached, instead of having to drink it out of a cup with no saucer, as though one were at Waterloo Station.

But that is an unworthy thought. For these milk-drinking moments are really among the happiest of my rather muddled life. The day is young, the house is quiet, the telephone has not yet begun to ring. Through my window I can see the massive branches of the old walnut tree, which time has moulded into a design of strong masculine beauty—one is reminded of muscled arms delighting in the exercise of their strength. And here, on the warm bed, bending over the tray, drinking his milk, is Oscar. The pink tongue darts in and out, making the pleasantest little splashing sound, the eyes are half closed in contentment, gradually the level of the milk sinks till the saucer is dry, and the splashing sound is replaced by two or three faintly rasping noises as he makes sure that the saucer is quite clean. After which, he sits up very straight, sniffs, and begins to wash his face, as all good cats should.

He is happy, I am happy, the whole world seems to be purring. Then the telephone starts to ring. And as I struggle out of bed to answer it I think how strange it is that we should spend our lives sweating and striving for this and that and the other when all we need is here at hand. A cat, a saucer of milk, a few blankets, and through the window the glimpse of a walnut tree lifting its limbs in delight to the clean, cold sky.

N stands for Neighbours.

Was Ham Common an F district? This was, of course, the first thing I wished to know when I was moving in.

To inquire of the house-agents would have been useless, as I knew from long experience. House-agents tell you everything except what you really want to know. Invariably they inform you that there is a 'wealth of old oak'. Never that there is a wealth of old cats.

By an F district I mean a district where on one's afternoon walks through the little Georgian streets that cluster by the river one would be privileged to see plump creatures sitting on doorsteps, and—by employing various cunning devices, such as twig-rattling, and key-jingling—entice them into a short session of general conversation. (These interludes are not always so tranquil as they sound. Sometimes the curtains of the house are drawn, and an angry woman looks out, with drawn brows, convinced that one is a cat-stealer.) I also mean a district where, while one is strolling in the shadow of a high garden wall, one may suddenly hear a strange, unearthly wail and—looking up—discover that Providence has provided one with a Siamese. Indeed, there is just such a walk in my neighbourhood, and I often wander past it in the hope that the resident Siamese may appear. But it seldom does so, and up till now it has remained regrettably aloof, not to say snooty. Part of the trouble is that the top of the wall is just too high for me to reach it. If it were lower I could startle it with a brilliant display of back-slappings and reverse whisker-strokings, at the same time murmuring, in a casual manner, that I happened to be the President of the Bexhill-on-Sea Cat Club, and that I was generally well thought of in the feline world. It gives me no opportunity to convey this information, and as far as it is concerned I might be nobody at all.

However, there are other feline neighbours, who are not so backward—and though it may seem outrageous to suggest that there could be *any* time in the life of a true F when the visits of *any* cat could be unwelcome—I must reluctantly confess that there have been moments when the visits of these neighbours have been embarrassing.

Which brings us to the Strange Case of 'Five' and The Toms.

This is a delicate matter.

For the trouble about 'Five' is that owing to his extreme prettiness, his bar-maid plumpness, and the way he rolls his enormous green eyes, he puts quite the wrong idea into the heads of the more rakish toms who roam the district. This results in situations of some difficulty. 'Five's' attitude is completely innocent; he is inviting no irregular responses; he is merely intrigued by the singular antics and caterwaulings of the large fierce creatures who come and serenade him. What can they possibly *mean*, these hoarse entreaties? Why all this fuss? These are the questions he asks himself, as he sits in all his plumpness and prettiness, rolling his eyes, within safe distance of the haven of the cat-door.

What does one do, in these circumstances? One cannot go out and read them the Wolfenden Report, because they would not understand it, and even if they did, it might only make matters worse. One cannot rush out and start shouting and throwing things, because any such behaviour would immediately be interpreted by 'Five', with his ultra-sensitive nature, as a reproach to himself, and he would only dart off and cower under a rhododendron, in a state of maidenly alarm. Which, in its turn, would probably inspire the toms with even more inflammatory notions.

What, in fact, I do is—talk. Casting a look of grave reproof at the tom, I lift up 'Five' and take him indoors, and sit him down and read him a quiet lecture. 'My dear "Five",' I begin ... but it would sound too idiotic if I were to put it into direct speech. The general purport is that he has led a very sheltered life, that this is a changing world, in which nothing is quite the same as it was, and in which people, and cats, often behave in a way which would have made our grandmothers turn in their graves. No blame, I assure him, attaches to anybody. Even the tom, if visited by a psychiatrist, would probably be informed that its behaviour was due to some quite common complex. All the same ... my dear 'Five' ... a simple life is usually happier than a complex one, so next time you see these serenading gentlemen do not roll your eyes at them. Just look the other way.

Apart from these problems, life goes by placidly enough, with only just enough drama to lend a spice of variety to the feline calendar. Our two nearest neighbours are Rudolph and Webster, in the cottage next door. Rudolph is ginger, with a temper to match—a most pep-

pery creature, though I hate to say it. We hardly know him, except as an orange streak, darting up the trunks of pear trees or shooting across the lawn, with a tail inflated like a fox's brush. Whenever Rudolph appears there is trouble.

Webster, on the other hand, is the gentlest of cats—a soft brown tabby with melting eyes. It says a great deal for the sweetness of his disposition that 'Four', 'Five', and Oscar have allowed him the freedom of the cat-door. No, perhaps that would be putting it too strongly; but at least they make no active protest when he appears. The drill is always the same. There is the sound of a 'plonk' outside as Webster jumps down from the lower roof of the tool-shed. A shadow falls across the cat-door. 'Four', 'Five', and Oscar, sitting with folded arms round the fire, exchange Looks. The cat-door creaks, as a brown paw is pushed through; there is a moment's pause, and then Webster's head appears, followed by his body. He gives a faint mew and then walks calmly—followed by the Looks—to the fish-plates under the sink, and proceeds to eat what is left. When I first saw this phenomenon I could hardly believe my eyes; cats are usually bitterly jealous of any violation of their domestic territory.

Webster is a car-sitter. On summer mornings, when I have left the car outside the garden gate over-night, I draw the curtains and look out, and there is Webster, stretched on the bonnet, basking in the sunshine. I have never fully understood this penchant, shared by so many cats, for the bonnets of cars. In cold weather, if a car had just been driven, there would be an obvious explanation—the warmth of the bonnet. But cats sit on cars in all weathers; never in my experience *in* them, of their own free will, though I believe that Siamese cats can be trained to do so.

Webster is also a post-sitter. He perches on one of the posts of the garden gate, and as he is very fat, with a large sit-upon, and as the post is very slender, he overlaps, so that he gives a strange effect of being impaled. How he manages to retain his balance in such a posture is a mystery.

From these brief notes it will be gathered that Webster has definitely come to stay.

And then there are 'Omo', 'Daz', and 'Tide'.

These are three snow-white kittens who have only recently come into my life. Perhaps it is not quite accurate to describe them as 'neighbours', because they live on the other side of the common, in a cottage so small that when the last white tail has vanished through the front-door you feel that the interior must be seriously over-crowded. The cottage belongs to an old lady whom some of my readers may have met before—Miss Mint.

Miss Mint is one of those gentle, unassuming women who always seem to attract to themselves the most extraordinary adventures. If there is a crook in the neighbourhood—and even in this predominantly Jane Austen locality crooks have been known to intrude—he makes straight for Miss Mint, and either borrows money or sells her something that does not work. If Borstal boys escape from homes of correction they make a bee-line over Miss Mint's fence. And if illegitimate babies are being deposited on local doorsteps, they are invariably deposited on Miss Mint. No ... I must not exaggerate. But since her arrival at the cottage, five years ago, there have been two such unexpected infants, one in a fully fledged pram and the other in a cardboard box, which is quite enough for a maiden lady with a taste for water-colours.

And if kittens are being abandoned ... but here again I must not exaggerate, for it has only happened once. The circumstances were such as would have appealed to any Victorian melodramatist. It was Christmas Eve; it was bitter cold, with a flurry of snow dusting the top of the laurel hedge; and there, on the doorstep, when Miss Mint returned from church, was a wicker laundry basket with the three white kittens. And lest your heart is wrung by the thought of them, shivering and deserted, they were reposing on an old plaid shawl wrapped round a hot water bottle, which was still warm.

I do not know enough about these three small bundles of enchantment, as yet, to recount any of their adventures. At the moment all I can say is that they are living up to their names in an uncanny manner, thereby justifying my theory that a name has a strange creative force of its own, which gradually imposes upon its owner a sort of psychic personality. If you have a female infant, and if you are so unkind as to baptize it Clara, a form of Clara it will become, which can hardly be any nice girl's ambition.

In the case of the kittens, 'Omo' really *does* 'add brightness to whiteness'; he is by far the perkiest. 'Daz' really *does* 'wash whitest of all'; at least, he washes longest, which in the case of a kitten is much the same thing. And 'Tide' is aptly named because this excellent detergent, as we all know, is blended with the mystic 'Bluinite'—a compound which for some reason or other I cannot discover in the Oxford Dictionary—and you can distinctly see specks of Bluinite in 'Tides's' eyes.

So there are our neighbours. Not a very large cast, I am afraid, but large enough. For a single cat, by the mystic force of its personality, can fill the largest stage.

O stands for Odes.

Most of the poets who have written verse about cats would have been better employed composing advertisements for detergents. Even Keats, in his sonnet 'To Mrs Reynolds's Cat' was only able to achieve a patronizing sneer:

> For all the wheezy asthma—and for all
> Thy tail's tip is nick'd off—and though the fists
> Of many a maid have given thee many a maul,
> Still is that fur as soft as when the lists
> In youth thou enter'dst on glass-bottled wall.

These lamentable lines stamp the author of the 'Ode to a Nightingale', for all time, as non-F. They are as cacophonous as any of the grunts coughed up by the spluttering pen of Robert Browning. Apart from that, they have a streak of insensitivity that mounts almost to sadism. Unless, of course, you think that the painful disease of asthma, in man or beast, is a fit subject for satire, or that there is anything amusing about the idea of young females 'mauling' defenceless animals.

Shelley was almost as bad, His 'Verses on a Cat' are so crude and ugly that they might have been written by the school bully. Wordsworth, by comparison, was almost F—there is a feline lilt and grace about his lines 'The Kitten and Falling Leaves'; but he gives himself away in the last five lines:

> What would little Tabby care
> For the plaudits of the crowd?
> Over-happy to be proud
> Over-wealthy in the treasure
> Of her own exceeding pleasure?

No F could have written those words. Little Tabby would have cared a great deal for the plaudits of the crowds. Of all animals cats are most conscious of their audience, and always give their best performances before a full house.

But the cat-poets reach their lowest level when they begin to symbolize, when they invest Felinity with ancient rites, mysteries, and what-have-you. One of the worst poems ever written, surely, must be Oscar Wilde's 'The Sphinx'. Listen to this:

> *Lift up your large black satin eyes which are like cushions where one sinks!*
> *Fawn at my feet, fantastic Sphinx! and sing me all your memories!*

No, Oscar, *no*! Cross it out, and throw it away, and call a hansom cab and take Lord Alfred out to luncheon at the Café Royal ... where, perhaps, after the third absinthe, you will say something delicious about the ortolans.

'*Cushions where one sinks*' indeed! Could the Rhyming Dictionary suggest no happier echo than that? The picture evoked by these words would have made an enchanting subject for Max; Wilde was a very heavy man and a great many cushions would have been necessary. As for 'fawning at his feet'—or rather at his side-buttoned, patent leather boots—never did the artful aids of alliteration lead an artist so astray. Even the humblest kitten from the alley would be outraged by an invitation to 'fawn'. Really, one would think that dear Oscar had been keeping company with corgis.

But sometimes, out of all this welter of inferior rhyming, a masterpiece emerges. Such is Thomas Hardy's 'Last Words to a Dumb Friend'—an elegy more moving than many that have been carved on the tombs of princes. And Swinburne, in his verses 'To a Cat', wrote as if he were addressing a creature of equal, though different, intelligence.

And here and there, as one thumbs the pages of feline literature, a little gleaming phrase shines out, like cats' eyes gleaming in the dark.

> Wind is a cat
> That prowls at night
> Now in a valley
> Now on a height
> It sings to the moon
> It scratches at doors;
> It lashes its tail
> Around chimneys and roars
> Then chasing the stars
> To the tops of the firs
> Curls down for a nap
> And purrs, and purrs.

I know nothing about the poet who created that charming conceit—Ethel Romig Fuller. But we will all agree that she was definitely F.

And so was another American—Helen Maring. She it was who wrote a poem which might be called 'the humblest poem ever written' . . . so tiny, so naïve, that it lives only through the virtue of its own humility. Why does it move me so? Listen:

> I have no pets to hold my heart
> No pets to fill a need:

But hungry creatures of the night
Come to my porch to feed . . .
No litter in the puppy's bed
No cat beside the fire,
Only the friends I do not see
To fill the deep desire.
The city's poor and hungry cats
Whose masters know the need.
I have no pets to hold my heart—
But little friends to feed.

Poetry? Perhaps not. Does it matter so much? For there is something greater than poetry, and that is compassion, which is the poetry of the human heart.

And yet, there *should* be great cat poetry. There should be triumphant Odes to Tabbies; there should be Sonnets to the Siamese; there should be Epics to the Unknown Heroes of the Alley.

Could we not write one ourselves? Could we not, for example, sit down at this very moment and write an ode to Oscar? Would it be so very difficult? After all, words are words, and one is used to adjusting them, and if one is presented with the extra puzzle of a rhyme, that should but add spice to the exercise. Even as I write, Oscar enters, rather solemnly, sits by the side of the waste-paper bas-

ket, and gazes up at me. I look into his eyes. So it shall be a poem to Oscar's eyes. We look at each other. I write . . .

In your eyes is a strange sea-changing
Green to gold and gold to grey,
Dark and swift as the west wind ranging
Over the breakers in the bay . . .
In your eyes there are ancient sorrows
Tears unshed for tales forlorn
Tales of all our lost tomorrows
All our yesterdays unborn.
In your eyes . . .

But no; a cobbler should stick to his last. It is sorry stuff. And yet, four words in that little jingle set me thinking, as though somebody else had written them. Our 'lost tomorrows' . . . our 'yesterdays unborn'. There is something there, some elusive truth that might be worth pursuing. There *are* tomorrows that may be lost . . . dawns on which we deliberately draw down the blinds. There are yesterdays, in which we live and have our being, though they never happened at all. It is all very confusing. Maybe a true poet could tell me what I am trying to say.

Oscar knows, of course. But Oscar is keeping his own counsel.

P stands for Power.

'*Power tends to corrupt and absolute power corrupts absolutely.*' LORD ACTON

This sombre generalization has been quoted so often before that you may wonder why I should quote it again, particularly in these light-hearted pages. It has been the theme of countless essays for school-boys and undergraduates. In the 'thirties, during the rise of Hitler and Mussolini, it was set up in permanent type in the offices of our great newspapers. The leader-writers would have been lost without it.

But always it has been applied to *men*. It has been used as a sort of yardstick to measure the pace of a dictator's decadence. A very efficient yardstick it has proved to be, historically; with its assistance you can trace the gradual hardening of the lines in a 'great' man's face, the slow, cruel ossification of the hands that hold the reins of authority.

Nobody, as far as I am aware, has yet applied this grim truth to the relationship of man with the animal kingdom. It is about time that somebody did so.

Consider an extreme example—the lion-tamer in the circus, an institution which I have attacked before and shall attack again. This is probably bad policy for any writer; not only does he incur the displeasure of one of the most powerful vested interests in the entertainment industry but he invites the attention of a very special brand of animal lunatic. I know this from bitter experience. Whenever I have breathed a word of criticism of circuses, shoals of protesting letters have arrived. 'But the elephants *love* being made to stand on their heads! And the dear little dogs *adore* being made to walk the tight rope in pink silk trousers with a spotlight in the eyes, night after night! And the ponies would feel positively *miserable* if they were just running round the fields instead of waltzing backwards in front of a deafening brass band! As for the lions ...'

Let us get back to those lions and the men who put them through their paces. Let us see this beastly business in its true light.

A lion is a cat. A very large cat, that has the power of inflicting death on a man.

Death can only be matched by death, and that—when all the trimmings are off—is the basis of the lion-tamer's little game. He makes the lion perform, for profit, under the constant threat of death. And the lion knows it. He is reminded of it by a thousand prods and insults and cuts and lashes. He roars his protests, he makes clumsy, futile gestures with his giant paws, there is a blazing grief in his tormented eyes, but he goes through with the act. Because he does not want to die. Even in the glaring lights, amid this bewildering uproar, subjected to a physical and psychological torture that makes the methods of the Gestapo seem comparatively humane, he is still alive, and life is sweet, or could be. And for that reason, and for that reason only, he does not leap off his stool and hurl himself in a single lethal avenging blow at the ugly little puppet who has taken command of his life.

Anybody who denies these obvious—and to me, very moderate—arguments, should have his head examined. And even more, his heart. The circus is an institution which should long ago have vanished from any enlightened society, and the profession of lion-taming should long ago have been abolished by law, together with such comparatively respectable callings as drug-peddling and white slavery.

There we go again! Getting all hot under the collar, when really we only set out to amuse. Which is why no work of mine will ever be what the critics call an 'artistic unity'.

To relieve the tension, let us leave the stench and uproar of these vicious places, and return to the quiet green lawn. And let us reduce the scale of the picture, and turn the lion into a cat. The lesson is still the same, even if it is in terms of comedy instead of tragedy.

Can you imagine calling a cat to 'heel'? One's mind boggles at the prospect. Supposing I were walking across the lawn with 'Five', and I suddenly called 'Heel,' what would happen? 'Five' would stop in his tracks and very slowly turn his head, and regard me with an expression of the utmost astonishment. What *was* that strange word? And to whom was it addressed? If he were in an amiable mood, the look of astonishment would be tempered by pity. Perhaps I am feeling unwell? Perhaps the sound 'heel' . . . unless he misinterpreted it . . . was some strange form of human hiccup? If that were the case, his natural kindness, and feline etiquette, instructs him to ignore it. And so, with a faint shrug, he would resume his walk, holding his tail very erect, in the assured conviction that where *he* leads, I will follow.

This seems to me precisely as it should be. It is the only proper relationship between a human being and an animal. Anybody . . . but *anybody* . . . any lout, any half-wit, any scruffy, self-centred moron, can command the affection and the servile obedience of a dog, but it takes intelligence and understanding—sometimes I think a certain psychic rapport—to win the affection of a cat. As for obedience, you will never get it, and if you are even faintly worthy of the honourable title of F, you will never want it. This is probably the root difference between those who are 'pro-dog' or 'pro-cat'. I am 'pro' practically anything on four legs except snakes, which is perhaps not quite how I meant to put it, but we will let it stand. But the reason why I and my fellow Fs tend more to the feline than the canine is basically because we have a greater respect for the whole animal kingdom.

In case this makes a number of tweedy ladies snort with such loud indignation that their corgis rise from the hearth-rug in dismay and take refuge in the gun-room—I am assuming that such barbaric strongholds still exist—let me ask them a question. Have they never felt even a faint shiver of disquiet at the sight of a man with a well-trained dog? A nice young man in tweeds, with a pipe and a good pair of calves, going for a walk across the common with a pedigree Alsatian? Does such a spectacle arouse no feelings of alarm and despondency? Do they see it all from the outside, as a simple picture of normal outdoor English life?

I don't. And in case the tweedy ones think that this must indicate some form of moral perversity, let them look at the picture through my eyes.

There he goes, our young man with the Alsatian, and how bravely he struts along with the dog frisking beside him! How proudly he holds his head, with this comical slave at his side!

But then, he nears the main road. Suddenly, things are different. He snaps 'Heel.' And the dog, if it is a good dog, comes to heel. But as it does so, it cringes, with its tail between its legs. It is a good dog, a well-treated dog, fed on the best biscuits, tended by the best vet., adored by the family. And no doubt the young man is a good young man, as straight as a die, a faithful husband, a loving father, with all the approved instincts. One of the best.

The fact remains that the relationship between him and his dog is a slave relationship, and is *ipso facto* corrupt. If I were to read this statement to the Canine Committee of the local Rotary Club there would probably be a great deal of raising of hairy eyebrows.

And now the tweedy ones can go off to their gun-rooms, and extract their corgis from behind their husbands' macintoshes, where they will doubtless be cowering, and take the ecstatic creatures for a walk. But when they call their dogs to 'heel', I hope that they will not snap the word with quite such assurance, as though they had a divine right to use it, merely because they have two legs instead of four. It is not a pretty word and what it stands for is in no way commendable. Lord Acton knew what he was talking about.

Q stands for Quiz.

All conscientious Fs from time to time should do a little mental stock-taking, in order to assure themselves that they are not growing lax, and that their standards are not slipping. The following simple test will help them to assess their own qualifications correctly. It is composed on the familiar lines of the popular quiz game, which is usually devoted to less important subjects.

Each question has four alternative answers, and each answer is marked with a corresponding letter, A, B, C, or D. These letters entitle you to certain marks—3, 2, 1, or 0. Take a sheet of paper, and answer questions with complete honesty, writing down your various As, Bs, Cs, or Ds. Then turn to the end of the chapter, where you will find what each answer is worth in terms of marks. Add them all up, and you will find your correct F category.

I hope that the above paragraph makes sense; I have been tying myself up in knots for the past half-hour, trying to make it clear. Arithmetic was never my strong point.

Here goes:

1. *If you are lunching alone on casserole of chicken, and if pussy enters the room at precisely the moment when you remove the lid—as she almost certainly will—what do you do?*

A. Shoo her away?

B. Extract a piece of chicken, put it on a side-plate, cut it up, blow on it—in a genteel fashion—and then present it to pussy?

C. Mix some gravy with some bread and put it aside to cool?

D. Take out a small portion, such as a giblet, and place it before pussy on the carpet?

2. *If pussy is lost, what do you do?*

(In asking this question I am assuming that you live in surroundings where there is at least some access to the outside world, even if it is only over the wall into your neighbour's back garden. Also that pussy has been lost for at least six hours.)

A. Ring up the police?

B. Stand at the back door calling 'Puss puss'?

C. Patrol the district with a tin plate, tapping it with a fork to simulate a dinner gong, at the same time ringing your neighbours' doorbells to inquire if they have seen a tabby with a smudge on its nose?

D. Trust in God and read Psalm 23?

3. *If pussy is sick on the carpet, what do you do?*

A. Ring the bell for Gaskin?

B. Clear it up with a shovel and when you next meet pussy, greet her with a scowl?

C. Clear it up with last week's copy of the *News of the World*, sigh, and when you next meet pussy greet her with a sympathetic smile and a stroke, but only a very tentative one, in case she might do it again on the linoleum?

D. Examine the unpleasant evidence, for traces of fur or other irritants, clear it up, go out into the larder to sniff the fish saucepan, and ... if the results of these tests are negative ... make a note on your pad to ring up the vet?

4. *If you are visited by a non-F friend who dislikes cats, what do you do?* (I don't mean a person who has a genuine neurasthenic cat-phobia—merely somebody who shoos them away.)
A. Do you politely remove pussy from the room?
B. Do you endeavour to reason with the non-F, informing her that cats are really 'just as intelligent or devoted as dogs'?
C. Do you allow things to take their course, in the faintly malicious hope that pussy may spring on the non-F's lap?
D. Do you keep pussy firmly on your own lap, and ask the non-F if she would be so kind as to pour out the tea?

5. *If pussy is fighting another pussy, what do you do?*
A. Ring for Gaskin and rush upstairs for the aspirin?
B. Shout and roar and hurl small clods of earth?
C. Intervene at all costs, even if it means climbing into the next garden?
D. Nothing?

6. *If pussy refuses to eat her fish, what do you do?*
(I am assuming, of course, that the fish is fresh and that pussy's nose is cold and her fur is in good shape and that there are no signs of physical or mental indisposition.)
A. Speak to her severely, telling her that she will get no more until she has eaten this lot?
B. Put the fish on a clean plate, rearrange it in a different pattern, and then take pussy for a walk in the garden in the hope that nature will eventually take its course?
C. Cook another lot of fish?
D. Open a tin of cat's meat?

So much for the questions. Now for the answers. The maximum score is 18, so anything above 15 may be regarded as excellent. From 15 to 12 is quite good. From 12 to 9 is doubtful. Below 9 is beyond hope.

	A	B	C	D
Question 1	0	3	1	2
Question 2	1	2	3	0
Question 3	1	0	2	3
Question 4	3	0	1	2
Question 5	1	2	3	0
Question 6	0	3	2	1

I trust that most Fs will agree with the marks that I have assigned to their answers. However, there are two cases in which there may perhaps be some grounds for argument.

The first is in question 4, which deals with the problem of what to do when visited by a non-F. I have given top marks to the person who 'politely removes pussy from the room'. This may seem an unwarranted surrender to non-Fness, but as the result of long and earnest consideration I have decided that this is the best course. The non-F will only bore pussy, and pussy will make the non-F feel ill at ease.

After all, in our dealings with non-Fs we must never forget that their non-Fness is not their own fault; they were just made that way. It is an affliction rather than a crime, and we must always be very nice to them. Speak to non-Fs gently and always open the door for them when they leave the room—which one hopes they will do as soon as possible. If the subject of Fness crops up, brush it aside, as one would if an unmusical person were to express an opinion about Bach.

The other marking which may be contested is 3 for B in question 6—about putting the fish on a clean plate, rearranging it in a different pattern, and then taking pussy for a walk in the garden. Some Fs. may consider that the award should more properly have gone to C—'Cook another lot of fish.' But I feel very strongly that B is right.

It is a question of feline psychology. Granted that pussy is in good health, that the fish is fresh and served at the proper time, the reason for pussy's refusal to eat is almost certainly psychological. For instance, at precisely the moment when she was about to take the first bite, the dustman may have clattered past, causing alarm and creating a temporary complex. Or there may have been some disturbing domestic incident such as the changing of a piece of furniture. We may, perhaps, have moved her armchair to another part of the room without previously consulting her, and this she naturally finds very strange behaviour and not at all the thing; she must express her disapproval in some way or other. People must learn. The fish must be loftily ignored.

All such temporary upsets can quickly be cured by a walk in the garden, accompanied by tactful strokings and twiddlings of twigs. By the time we return to the kitchen, where the newly arranged fish is waiting on a clean plate, pussy will almost certainly have regained her appetite.

R stands for Rain (and wind and snow).

If animals walk with you through life, if they are by your side not only as casual callers but as constant companions, inevitably they affect your way of thinking and—I hope—sharpen your understanding.

Thus it is with the weather. When I wake up on a winter's morning, and find that the wind has risen during the night, and is rattling at the windows, wailing down the chimney, making the old branches of the walnut tree creak in protest, the first thing I think is, 'This will drive "Five" crazy.'

I think of other things, of course—sailors at sea, and the breakers battering their white fists against the Cornish rocks; and—to come nearer home—the inadequacy of the stakes supporting the latest batch of conifers in the garden. I foresee a busy morning, balancing on steps and hammering, and stamping the earth more firmly round the aching roots.

But first of all I think of 'Five'. None of the cats is quite normal when the wind is high, but 'Five' seems to lose his head completely. It is as though he heard, in the uproar around him, the clank of ghostly dustbins. Even as I lie in bed I know that he will be in and out of it all, making dramatic entrances and exits through the cat-door, and scampering wildly across the lawn to the pear tree, where he will sharpen his claws against the unseen enemies that the wind always seems to bring.

And thus again it is with the rain. To non-Fs, rain may mean macintoshes and dirty boots and colds in the head and leaks in the larder. To true Fs it means paw marks. If the rain keeps on—and for the sake of the aforesaid conifers we may well hope that it does—there will be paw marks all over the house. On the window-sills, round the fish plates under the sink, in the bath, on the draining board, and—of course—firmly printed across the papers on my desk. Fs do not resent these paw marks; on the contrary, they welcome them. If I were the sort of person who wrote for posterity, I might harbour flattering thoughts about those paw marks, picturing the puzzlement of some critic unborn as he bent over these ghostly symbols, bespattering the dusty pages. However, I have often had a notion that the authors who court the critics of tomorrow have seldom been kindly received by the critics of today. Present popularity, whatever the intelligentsia may say to the contrary, is not always the prelude to future oblivion.

None of this is very apposite to the theme which we are developing, so let us content ourselves by noting that my own manuscripts go straight into the waste-paper basket, Oscar's paw marks and all.

Cats even invest a fall of snow with an extra magic. The afternoon grows chill and sullen, the skies darken before their time, and in the air is the curious scent that means snow is on its way. On the following morning one looks out of the window on to the exquisite transformation scene which—though I am old enough to know better—never fails to give me the same sort of thrill as one had at one's first pantomime, when the curtain rose on a stage glittering white, with a diamond palace whose towers reached up to a sky ablaze with silver sequins.

As soon as breakfast is over one wraps up and pulls on gum-boots, filled with excitement at the thought of all that is waiting in the Arctic world outside. The camellias will be the first port of call, in order that the weight of snow may be shaken from their branches; there was once a sad occasion when one of my best camellias was split clean in half after a heavy fall. Then we must go to the tool-shed for a long broom, and over to the greenhouse to scrape the snow from the roof. This, I freely admit, I do for the sheer fun of it. There is something oddly satisfactory about scraping snow from a greenhouse roof, hearing it 'plonk' down to the earth, and watching the inside of the greenhouse, which had been cloaked and shadowed, come back to life as the sun floods in again through the clear glass. Yes, it will be an exciting morning.

But look! As we step out of the porch, relishing the crunch of snow beneath our feet, which is unlike any other sound in nature, we see that somebody has been here before us—in fact, several somebodies. Three sets of paw prints start at the base of the walnut tree and then fan out to the north, the east and the west. On this immaculate surface they have a carven delicacy, as though the cats had been treading with special care and elegance. How wonderful it would be to shrink, to become small and furry, to find oneself in the proud possession of a tail, and to start stalking those prints! Each of them, we may be sure, could tell a tale of adventure.

Indeed, even as we stand there staring we shall find that if we let our eyes follow the track leading to the north it will conduct us to the old pear tree. And there, high up in the fork, is 'Five'.

He is looking madder than ever, with his ears at the alert, and his fur fluffed out against the cold, and he is turning his head this way and that as though he had never seen a fall of snow before. Usually when any of the cats is stationed in the fork of the pear tree it is a sign that dalliance is demanded, and one must go in search of leaves and twigs to twiddle before them. Not today. All one's efforts would be ignored; there are too many counter-attractions, highlighted by the snow. The occasional blackbird, making his swift staccato progress across the dazzling white, looks bigger and blacker than ever before, and the tracks he leaves, like carelessly scribbled phrases of music, must be terribly tantalizing. And then, with each breath of the wind, a little flurry of snowflakes flutters down from the upper branches, and to 'Five', dabbing at them with his paw, they must seem like the white petals that he chases over the lawn in the winds of June, or the white butterflies that he stalks in summer as they hover over the purple panicles of the buddleia.

The snow and the storm, the sun and the shadow, the wind and the rain . . . these can mean little to the city dweller, imprisoned in his concrete tomb; to the countryman they are a dominating theme in the whole pattern of his existence. And to the countryman who is also an F, the Theme has infinite variations.

S stands for Solitude.

A sad section, this.

Last night I had to go to the opera. There I was at seven o'clock, all dressed up in the hall, looking into the mirror and tucking in my scarf. And suddenly, in the mirror I saw Oscar.

He was lying at the bottom of the stairs, watching me, in an attitude of the most poignant allurement. His front paws were dangling over his chest, his eyes were swimming with emotion, and now and then his tail did a little twitch.

I stopped fiddling with my scarf, and stared at Oscar's reflection. The house was very silent. Then Oscar spoke. And this is what he said:

'Must you go out? Have you thought of *me*? When you have gone, when the front door has slammed and when the sound of your motor car has echoed into the distance, what shall I do? It is too cold to walk in the garden. I cannot stare at one of those strange bundles with fluttering pages which you call "books". There are no mice in the wainscot; those were disposed of years ago. You suggest that I might take a bath? But I have washed myself till my tongue aches. Or that I might go to sleep? But I have slept till I am weary of sleeping.

'So what shall I do? If I were in the jungle, where I really belong, there would be lots to do. Lots that I should *have* to do. I should have to hunt for food, and search for shelter; I might even have to fight for my life. Which would be very painful and exhausting, but at least it would be *living*. But you have relieved me of all those necessities; you have given me a home, and comfort, and two meals a day, and you have breathed something of your spirit into me. As a result, I am no longer a cat, pure and simple; I am to some extent a human being, with some of your own feelings and some of your own pleasures . . . and many of your ennuis.

'So please tell me, what shall I *do*?'

That is what Oscar is saying, as he lies there, glancing from me to the door, and making these small gestures of entreaty. And I hope nobody will suggest that it is foolish to endow animals with the power of speech. They *do* speak, to those who they think will understand. Sometimes what they are saying makes very painful hearing.

So what do I do myself, in these circumstances? Obviously, I harden my heart, and go to the opera. But some of the pleasure has gone, as I think of that small creature, waiting in the hall. I wish I could have taken him with me.

And that starts a whole new line of thought.

If only I *could* take Oscar to the opera! He would, needless to say, outshine any other member of the audience. We would sit in the Royal Box and he would perch on the edge, in a small but exquisite diamanté cloak. And should Madame Callas have an off-night and sing a little sharp, Oscar would sit up and sing a little sharper. And the great audience would stare up to the box and there would be nudgings and whisperings and wild questionings. 'Who is that ravishing creature in the Royal Box? It cannot possibly be Princess Grace, because tonight she is opening something in Monte Carlo. It must certainly be *somebody* royal . . . such majesty, such grace, such condescension!' And Oscar, who would of course be aware of the sensation he was causing, would gently incline his head and give a flick to his diamanté tail.

If only I could take 'Four' as well!

In his case, the problem of solitude is even more acute because, as we have already seen, 'Four' is the Cat Who Does the Act, and when he is not receiving attention he does not merely look sad, like Oscar, he invests the occasion with the most poignant drama.

This is what happens. I sit at my desk, engaged in the daily pursuit of telling stories, which is not always as simple as it sounds. The scene is set; things are just beginning to get under way; people are moving and speaking naturally on the foolscap. Then there is a faint scratch on the door. I try to pretend that I do not hear it, but a moment later the scratch is repeated, not quite so faintly. There is nothing for it but to get up and open the door, hoping, as I do so, that this will be merely a brief interruption, a routine visit during 'Four's' morning tour of inspection.

But as soon as he stalks into the room I observe with dismay that this is to be no casual call. 'Four' is 'drenched'.[1] Everything proclaims it. The way he weaves round the waste-paper basket; the way his tail flicks; the curious ecstatic *vibrato* of his purr; the manner in which he rubs against my legs and regards me with liquid adoration.

Who could ignore such demonstrations? One cannot give him a swift pat and tell him to go away. Still less can one shoo him out and slam the door. The consequences of *that* would be too dreadful to contemplate! He would rush from the house in high drama, his green eyes lit with anguish, his fur—metaphorically—waving in the wind like widow's weeds. Though he would not actually clasp his paws to his bosom, his high level of dramatic technique would enable him to convey this effect. And for days on end the house and garden would become a place of feline reproach, with 'Four' crouching in the shadow of the woodpile, or curled on a cold shelf in the tool-shed ... 'Four' in his role of the outcast, the unwanted.

The reader will observe that there is not quite the same poignancy about the loneliness of 'Four' as the loneliness of Oscar. ('Five', thank heavens, is reasonably self-contained.) But though there is always something ever so faintly 'ham' about 'Four's' public appearances,

[1] 'Drenched' is an expression used by Fs to indicate a condition of deep affection, which is outwardly demonstrated by cats in the manner suggested above.

there is nothing bogus about his affection. When he visits me at these awkward hours in my study I see him as a little creature who has sought me out because, for the moment at least, I am the most important thing in his small world. He is telling me so, beyond any question, by the music of his purring, by the weaving of his small black body, by the light in his uplifted eyes. And what choice have I but to respond?

All the same, there have been many times in my life—and doubtless there will be many more—when I wished, most earnestly, that cats could read.

T stands for Telly.

All my cats are keen 'viewers'—rather a common word, I always think, but it seems to have come to stay.

'Four' and 'Five' patronize Gaskin's set, because Gaskin is rather grand about commercial television, and prefers to tune in to the B.B.C. 'Four' and 'Five' share his tastes; there are fewer Westerns on the B.B.C. and the bangs make them nervous.

A very soothing sight it is, of an evening, with 'Four' on Gaskin's lap and 'Five' stretched flat out on the table in the middle of the little room, his ears at the alert and his green eyes focused on the flickering screen. This position is revealing. We have already noted that owing to an unfortunate episode in his youth, 'Five' likes, whenever possible, to repose himself in strategic places, where he cannot be come upon unawares. And I am sure that he has chosen the eminence of the table because of a secret fear that some day one of the monsters of the screen—such as a crooner—might come to life, and burst through the frame, and roar at him. This is a fear to which I am subject myself. I would not at all mind if *some* of the pictures came to life—if, for example, the magic box were suddenly to break open during one of the African scenes, and discharge a glorious collection of antelopes and giraffes. But if this phenomenon were to occur at a moment when Miss Never Mind Who was singing one of her pop numbers, I should feel very differently. To find oneself face to face with a female crooner, roaring at one with her bared fangs and lashing her bespangled behind, would be a fate worse than death. And please do not tell me that female crooners cannot 'lash' their behinds. They can, and do, with immense profit to themselves.

Upstairs the scene is equally peaceful. I sit on the sofa, by a log fire, with Oscar as companion. At the beginning of the entertainment, he usually disposes himself on my knees, facing the set, in a Sphinx-like posture. Then, as the drama quickens, his front claws gradually emerge, and I have a sensation of walking through a bush of exceptionally thorny brambles. I bear this for as long as possible, for I know that it is not a sign of hostility but a token of deep regard; however, the time comes when he must be gently detached, and persuaded to lie by my side. If this is done firmly, and if it is accompanied by suitable expressions of regret, the transition is effected without embarrassment on either side.

I often wonder what animals actually *see* when they are watching the moving screen. Obviously, in the case of static pictures, their eyes do not register any connection between the photograph and the original. The royal corgis, should they happen to open the pages of the *Tatler*, would not yelp with joy at the sight of themselves arriving at Euston station, as they so often do; and 'Five', should he chance upon a picture of myself in a less exalted journal, would probably sit on it. Nor do statues interest them. I once had a rather sinister stork, in lead, which had been wished upon me by a charming old lady, now deceased. It was destined for the water-garden, and I felt obliged to put it there, to please her. It would not be so long before it was largely obscured by a cluster of *onoclea sensibilis*, and in the meantime it might amuse the cats. It did not amuse them at all. They spurned it; you would have thought they were deliberately cutting it. The stork is now in the gardens of a maternity hospital, striking terror into the hearts of the inmates.

Their swiftest response, of course, is to sound. At the barking of a dog they are immediately on the alert, and at the sound of birds calling—*real* birds—their tails begin to lash. They pay no heed to synthetic bird song. By this I mean the strange medleys of trills and

twitters, preserved on gramophone records, which accompany so many of the more sentimental moments of television drama. The play is nearly over ... the night is done and dawn is breaking. The hero and the heroine, once more united, stand at a window, arm in arm, staring with bright eyes at a new world. Cue for trills and twitters. Even if the action takes place in a New York penthouse these tearful scenes are invariably played against a positive bedlam of bird song, made up of bogus thrushes and plastic larks. If the heroine happens also to be having a baby, the bird song is even more persistent, particularly if the baby is illegitimate, as it usually is. One would almost think that child-birth in the minds of television producers, was connected, in some obscure way, with ornithology.

We still have not answered the question of what cats actually *see*. I would give a great deal to know; cats' eyes are among the most beautiful and mysterious jewels of the animal kingdom, and if we could only look through them, though but for a few seconds, we should have a vision of another world. From the purely physical point of view I fancy they are somewhat short-sighted. Often, on summer afternoons, when I am sitting by the lily pond at the far end of the lawn, one of them will emerge from the porch in search of me, in order, no doubt, to give me the latest espionage report, or maybe to register some complaint about the cuisine. And there he will stand on the terrace, staring around, and looking straight in my direction. But he does not seem to see me, and it is not until I call or clap my hands that he proceeds to walk in my direction. I need hardly say that he never runs. To run would be contrary to every precept of feline etiquette. Dogs may run towards their masters, never cats. They walk, with the utmost delicacy and deliberation, and as they draw near, they begin to make polite small-talk in the form of a series of soft mews, which is a form of social prelude to more serious conversation.

But though they may be physically short-sighted, and though when they watch the television they may not connect the visual image with the human personality, they *do* watch, keenly and closely. And sometimes I think that, for them, this is a form of artistic appreciation. Maybe they are seeing the dramas of the screen transmuted into abstract patterns, from which they gain the same pleasure as we might gain from an impressionist picture, in which familiar shapes are shown in musical groups of significant form.

Or am I on quite the wrong track? As they sit there, my three Sphinxes, are they in fact gazing towards horizons, infinitely distant, which my eyes will never scan?

U stands for Understanding.

I have always had the feeling that if 'Four', 'Five', and Oscar were to drink some magic potion which suddenly made them swell up to twenty times their natural size—till they were indeed as large as lions—there would be no cause for alarm. True, I should be faintly worried by the thought of the fish bill, and I should be obliged to make immediate arrangements for the enlargement of the cat-doors. I might also feel a momentary dismay at the thought of the amount of sheer physical energy which would have to be expended, in the future, on such diversions as tummy-rubbing, tail-pulling, and reversed whisker-stroking. The cats, remembering the techniques of the past, might find my efforts feeble and trifling.

Apart from these fleeting anxieties, there would be no qualms. The complete trust and confidence which had been established over the years would not be affected. Mutual understanding is not a matter of size.

In this conviction I am confirmed by the most remarkable animal book ever written—*Born Free*, by Joy Adamson. If ever medals were struck for outstanding Fness, Mrs Adamson would certainly merit the supreme award, for it was she who reared Elsa the lion cub, and gained her love, and kept it. Never, as far as I am aware, has there been such a miraculous marriage of two worlds, the animal and the human; and yet, perhaps it should not be called 'miraculous'; if we had faith and love enough, this would be the way things were naturally intended and ordained.

These pages are not designed for religious discussion, but in this context I may perhaps be forgiven for suggesting that when St Paul wrote of the faith that 'could remove mountains' he meant precisely what he said. It is merely a question of degree. I am among those who are fortunate enough to have seen the power of one man's thought acting on another man's body, acting instantly and physically, causing nerves and muscles to react in a way which would be totally impossible of their own volition. If faith can go so far, it can go infinitely further. It can direct not only the bodies of men but all the bodies in the animal kingdom. There are—quite literally—no limits to its power.

Faith is merely a facet of love—the love of God. If you had enough of it, you could walk into the cage of the fiercest lion and sleep by its side. Once again, it is a question of degree. Perhaps the caged lion is an unhappy example, for it has been surrounded since birth by human hatred and mockery, so that its eyes are clouded and its heart is hardened. But with a lion with whose mind you are in harmony, or indeed with any animal, you can speak with love and your love will be returned.

No sooner had I written those words than there was a mew at the door . . . Oscar's mew. Entering, he sat down, gazed up at me, and mewed again. He has about six basic mews, on which he plays many delicate variations. This was number 3, in D flat, which, being interpreted, meant: 'This is merely a social visit; I was passing, and I looked in to see how you were, and if you were working well.' To assure himself on this latter point he leapt on to the desk, and sniffed the manuscript. Then he leapt down again, and stalked out, tail erect.

I closed the door and went back to my desk. And then I saw that across the foolscap he had printed his signature of approval—three clearly defined prints of his four-padded paws. They were the prints of a domestic cat, yes. But they were also the prints of a jungle lion.

Before we leave this theme of 'Understanding', let us apply it to some practical purpose. Let us suppose that we are carrying a kitten round the garden for the first time, holding it closely in our arms, introducing it to the Great Outside. In order to perform this task successfully we must ourselves *become* kittens. Fs will of course understand this procedure, but non-Fs may suggest that it is (a) ridiculous and (b) impossible. We need not argue about whether it is ridiculous; it is certainly not impossible. Indeed, it is a most salutary exercise for any human being. The non-F might be interested in knowing how it is done. Here are the main outlines:

INSTRUCTIONS FOR TURNING ONESELF INTO A KITTEN

1. Refocus the eyes. This is partly a physical and partly a mental process. Physically it consists in throwing the head back and lowering the lids until the eyes are half closed. Mentally it means a quick Gulliver translation to the land of Brobdingnag, so that natural objects such as flowers and trees appear as the kitten sees them—the daffodils the size of poplars and the poplars the size of mountains.

2. Close the ears tightly for at least five minutes, at the same time keeping the eyes shut. This will sharpen the sense of hearing.

3. Blow the nose, rinse the nostrils in cold water, and take several deep sniffs of smelling salts. This will sharpen the sense of smell.

4. Make certain that you really *are* in Brobdingnag. There must be no half measures. It is no use keeping one foot, as it were, in this world. You must be so deeply in Brobdingnag that when you see a snowdrop you wonder if you would have the strength to saw

through the stalk and hoist it over your shoulder to carry it home. Having carried out these simple instructions you will be ready to carry the kitten round the garden. Naturally, since you are only a human being, and as such deficient in many of the finer animal senses, you will be at best a clumsy instrument. However, if you stay firmly in Brobdingnag, and if you keep your hand on the kitten's back as a sort of receiver through which to interpret its emotions, you should not do too badly.

V stands for Voices.

One of the sternest tests for those who wish to qualify as advanced Fs is that they should respond correctly to the sounds made by Siamese cats. Many Fs—they may otherwise be quite intelligent people, who would pass most of the tests, with the possible exception of reversed whisker-stroking—have faulty reactions in this important matter. They will say: 'Of course, I adore Siamese cats, but I do wish they wouldn't make that dreadful noise.'

Such an observation rules out, for ever, their chances of getting into the Alpha-plus class of Fness. The most they must hope for is an Alpha-minus, and even this would only be granted after a long course of correction.

For to the really advanced F the cry of the Siamese cat is one of the most beautiful sounds he can ever hear. In the whole symphony of nature there is only one sound with the same bitter-sweet timbre, and that is the cry of the seagull. Sometimes as I have sat on the cliffs of Land's End, watching the white patterns of their wings against the black seas below, listening to their voices echoing far and near, I have closed my eyes for a few moments and mentally transformed the seagulls into Siamese cats. What a paradise such a picture conjures up for the true F . . . what prospects of ineffable bliss! To find oneself in a world where the heavens were alive with flying pussies, swooping and wheeling above! To look up to the sky and see flocks of kittens scampering among the clouds . . . to look through the curtains as night falls and observe that the boughs of the old elm trees were no longer cluttered up with a lot of old rooks but weighed down under a vast, purring accumulation of beige fur, with hundreds of jewelled blue eyes twinkling in the dusk! It hardly bears thinking of.

But we were discussing voices. Why have we used the word 'voice' for this section, rather than the word 'mew'? Partly because many of the charming sounds made by cats bear no euphonic resemblance to a 'mew', still less to the ugly 'miaow' which is attributed to them by non-Fs. But mainly because a 'mew' is too often associated with sadness. When cats speak there is no reason to assume that they are saying something melancholy or making some complaint about life in general; indeed, the very reverse is often the case. For instance, Oscar greets me at least half a dozen times a day with a wide range of soft, husky sounds which are evidently signs of approval and affection, for they are accompanied by intermittent purrs, leg-weaving, and erect tail-waving, and while he makes them he gazes up at me with enormous liquid green eyes. I do not insult him by

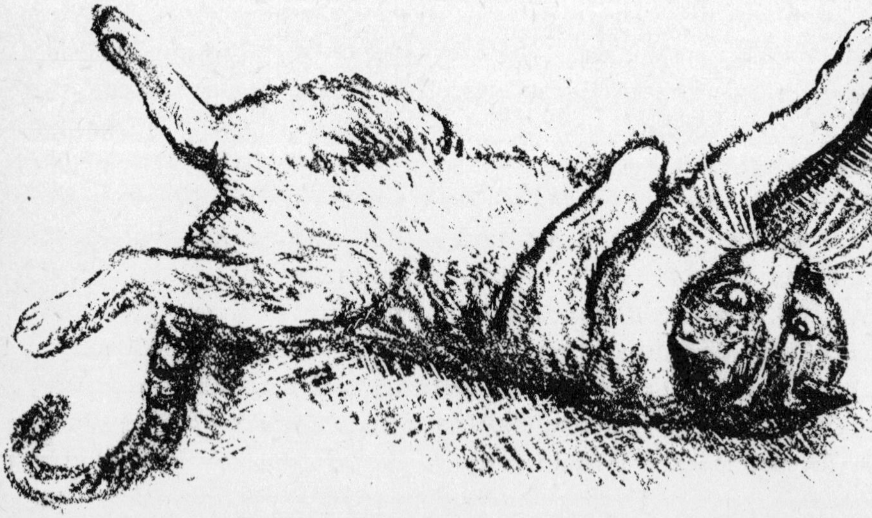

assuming that he is asking for another helping of fish; he is doing nothing of the sort; he is merely passing the time of day, inquiring after my mood, and making amiable small talk.

It is the same with 'Five', most of whose conversation is conducted while he is lying on his back, with his front paws dangling in front of him. 'Five' is perhaps a better listener than raconteur; he prefers that one should open the conversation, contenting himself with interjecting brief staccato comments when one pauses, which may be interpreted as 'Yes?' 'Indeed?' 'No!'

However, perhaps the most accomplished conversationalist is 'Four'. This is only to be expected, since he is the eldest, with the widest range of experience. He is, for example, the only cat of mine who has ever been lost.

And now that we have mentioned *that* appalling episode, which created a sensation in feline circles for a whole three days, perhaps I may be allowed to give my own theories about it, for the benefit of the future historian.

I have long had a suspicion, amounting almost to a certainty, that when 'Four' was lost it was all part of his Act. He was giving a supreme performance of his Role. Look at the facts, in case the data of this *cause célèbre* has momentarily slipped your memory. It happened at Merry Hall, in June. To be precise, on June 21st, which is the longest day in the year . . . and it certainly felt like it, by the time we all got to bed. There had been some argument about the fish: I have never been quite sure how it began, but Gaskin assures me that he did *not* begin it. However, it was enough to make 'Four' tap an impatient paw, and go into the first part of his act . . . dejection, terror, starvation, etc.

At this point, Cherry enters. Cherry is a very nice friend of Gaskin's, with grey hair, who makes—so we all understand—vast sums of money on the films playing distinguished diplomats. When he is not so employed he often comes down to sit in Gaskin's room and tell him stories of the great world which—judging by the hoarse peals of laughter echoing into my study—must sometimes be not a hundred miles removed from the knuckle.

Well, on this never-to-be-forgotten evening, Cherry suddenly

suggested that he should take 'Four' for a walk, and carry him in his arms for a short way down the lane, in order to coax him out of his Role. And since Cherry is F to the tips of his elegant fingers, Gaskin gave permission.

So out went Cherry, and scooped up 'Four', who by this time was heavily draped in the deepest *crêpe*. And down the lane he went, holding 'Four' very firmly and expertly, murmuring reassurances. You would think that 'Four' would have been flattered, but no. 'Four' was rigid. He said to himself . . . 'I am an artist. I have my role to consider. I will not be coaxed and wheedled by Mr Cherry, however much money he may be making. Apart from that, I have put on all this *crêpe* and an extra amount of eye-shadow and it is *not* going to be wasted.' (Those, I am convinced, were his very words.)

With which, he leapt from Cherry's arms into the hedge and completely disappeared for three whole days. But completely. We were up all night, and the next day, and the next two nights. The police were alerted, notices were posted all over the village, and though it would be an exaggeration to say that traffic was diverted, there were several times when I was nearly run over by the local delivery vans. If you stand in a country lane for hours on end, tapping a tin plate, you eventually get into a sort of daze.

And then, quite suddenly, without a word of explanation, 'Four' walked in through the front door. He was quite calm, his fur was sleek and glossy, and though he was perhaps not quite so plump he showed no particular eagerness to be served with his fish. He looked almost the same as on the night of his disappearance, with one highly

significant difference ... he had abandoned his *crêpe* and removed his make-up. And in his eyes was a tell-tale gleam of triumph—the triumph of an artist who has given a supreme performance and has reduced the entire audience to tears.

What all this has got to do with Voices I do not know. But I felt it necessary to give my own version of this drama, which has long been a subject of controversy in F circles.

W stands for Windows.

A tragic waif presses his nose against the window of my study. It is a bitter afternoon in December, and the shades of night are falling fast. There is a flurry of snow in the air, and the first flake falls on the waif's nose. The waif puts up his poor little paw to wipe it off. He shakes off the snow, and stays there on the window-ledge shivering ... staring into the brightly lit interior. His mouth opens in a mournful, silent mew.

It is all deeply moving. Like one of those Victorian illustrations to Dickensian novels, in which waifs, as such, seem to be permanently stationed outside the windows of the well-to-do in never-ceasing snow-storms, so that the plot may take its course.

The only fault with the picture is that it is completely bogus. For the name of the waif is Oscar. And Oscar is, at this moment, replete with a large whiting ... which can scarcely have been digested ... to say nothing of a bowl of milk, and various scraps of sweetbread from my own luncheon. Apart from that, there is a cat-door, just round the corner, waiting to welcome him. To say nothing of the window of the upstairs loo ... the one that we must get the carpenter to see to, because the branches of the wistaria are making it difficult to close.

As if this were not enough, he has already been in and out of the door of the porch at least three times in the last ten minutes. He has entered the room, tail erect, marched to the porch, and mewed to go out. Sighing deeply, and wondering how I ever manage to write anything more sustained than a motto for a Christmas cracker, I have risen from my desk and opened the door. A chill blast has blown in, swelling out the curtains, and sweeping the carefully arranged Christmas cards from the mantelpiece. Oscar exits. I go back to my desk. A minute later, he is back on the outside window-ledge, in his deepest waif make-up, and his mouth is once more opening in that mute, heart-rending mew. It is quite maddening, and I could not enjoy it more. And of course, I let him in.

So perhaps this should have gone into a section on Teasing, for no other interpretation can explain Oscar's singular behaviour. He is a highly intelligent cat; he knows all about the loo window and the cat-door. Indeed, the mellow rusty creak of the cat-door, swinging to and fro throughout the day as he makes his mysterious exits and entrances, is one of the happier echoes in the quiet domestic symphony of my life.

If I ever had to make a sort of surrealist gramophone record giving a composite sound picture of my ideal existence (there would probably be a very small sale for it) the *motif* of the cat-door would constantly recur, in a brisk tempo. Then there would be many sustained passages on the woodwind, to interpret the evening breeze as it sighs through the copper beech. And the soft silver 'toot' of the kettle as it reaches the boil in the tiny cottage over the way, punctually every afternoon at five minutes past four. And the hail on the roof of the greenhouse when one has been caught inside it during an April shower. And the thud of apples on a sun-parched lawn, and the rattle of walnuts on the roof of the tool-shed, and the petulant 'chuff-chuff' of the squirrels when one slaps one's hands in a futile effort to make them go away, so that one might have at any rate a few handfuls of one's own walnuts at Christmas. The rattle of the walnuts would be almost the only percussion in my modest symphony; there is quite enough percussion in the world without adding to it.

Indeed, I should be sparing even in my allotment of bird song.

I should of course include the two linnets who always serenade each other across the lawn in June—one from the pear tree and the other from the apple; and I might make very effective use of the screech owls who sound their eerie calls at midnight just outside my bedroom window. They give one a most agreeable *frisson*, and encourage one to believe in witches and evil spirits, which is, I think, an excellent idea, because the man who does not believe in evil spirits is unlikely to believe in good ones. But I should soft-pedal the black-

birds, who can be extremely annoying when one is trying out a tune in C major and they chatter away just outside the window in a nagging D sharp.

'Outside the window'—the phrase reminds me of what I began to write about—windows and Oscar's wickedness in demanding that they should be opened for him. There is a very special window noise associated with Oscar which would certainly be included in my symphony . . . the sound of his paw scraping on the glass of my bedroom window round about 7.20 a.m., just after he has had his fish in the kitchen. Why he has to tell me about it, wafting affectionate breaths of whiting over my pillow, I do not know, and why he has to come over the roof to do it, and print large black paw marks on my sheets, I do not know either. But I do know that I should miss these little visits very much; I hope it will be many a day before I reach out a sleepy hand to feel the comfort of his furry body, and find only an empty sheet.

I wish that my windows could be always open, on to the jungles and the prairies, on to the mean city streets, so that there might be a perpetual coming and going, a never-ceasing leaping and purring and scrambling into my small abode. But I am afraid that Gaskin might object. Three cats and one bachelor, he has sometimes hinted, are enough. He must be growing old.

XYZ

The End.

I hope that the reader will not be offended if I turn away from him, at this last moment, and address myself to the three small creatures who have been our companions throughout these pages.

I want to write them a letter. It is monstrous that one cannot write letters to one's cats. Often, when I have been abroad, I have wandered down some nice little winding street in a Mediterranean port, and paused at a kiosk to look at the picture postcards. And there I have seen some deliciously shiny ultramarine concoction showing a lot of tumbled houses, reeling up a hill, with my hotel on the top. And I have longed to buy it and post it to 'Five', scribbling ...

Dear 'Five',

X marks my bedroom and there is a very nice balcony which you would enjoy. The fish is very good, but rather bony. There are a great many cats who send their love. I am afraid that they are rather bony too. However, I am taking some of them out to dinner tonight, so I hope they will not be quite so thin tomorrow. I hope you are being a good cat, and looking after Gaskin. With much love and tell 'Four' and Oscar that I will be writing to them very soon.

B.N.

That is the sort of postcard that I would like to write, but somehow it never got itself written. So now we will make amends.

Dear 'Four',
Dear 'Five',
Dear Oscar,

We have been together, now, for quite a number of years. To you, it must have seemed even longer than to me, for you are cats and I am only a man. And seven years in your life—so we are given to understand—are equal to only one in mine.

Which means that you, my dear 'Four', are nearly 98. And I do wish that you would sometimes remember it, and not go rushing up the pear tree like a stripling, in order to sit there, and dab at the blossom, and roll your eyes so coyly. I must remind you that the old lady who lives next door is only 82, and she would never dream of behaving in such a manner.

This is a letter of thanks—the sort of thanks that really do come 'from the bottom of my heart'. The non-F would probably say that no thanks were due; he would say that I had given you a good home, and that was an end of it. I hope it is true that you have had a good home. But I do not have to be reminded that it has always been *my* home—I have dictated the moves, and settled the localities, without consulting you. True, I would have consulted you, had I been able. True, again, I have tried never to go to a place where you would be unhappy. Even during that dreadful year when the gods drove me mad, and chased me back to London, there was a large garden. The fact remains that you always had to follow where I led. One day, you would be happily wandering about in familiar territory, and the next you would suddenly find yourself shut in a basket, amid an uproar of frightening sounds and smells, and dragged away from your beloved trees and lawns. And when you stepped out of the basket, cramped and frightened, you always stepped into a new world. And you had to begin all over again.

Yet you never complained. You never looked at me reproachfully, asking me: 'What right have *you* to disrupt our lives like this? Who are *you* that you should assume these dictatorial powers?' Maybe you did not ask these questions because you sensed that it had not really been my fault; maybe you knew that I had not been acting wilfully but under those strange human compulsions, either of temperament

or of circumstance, that so often compel men to tear up the roots of their own true happiness. I hope that this was how you felt about it; I hope too that the roots have been torn up for the last time.

I find it hard to imagine life without you, without any one of you. If 'Four' were not, as it were, standing in the wings, waiting to do his act—and you know, my dear 'Four', it often *is* an act—I should feel that the drama of life had lost much of its savour. The day must come, I know, when 'Four' will play his last role, and I think that my heart will then tell me that he is no longer acting. I shall look into his eyes and I shall know. I would rather not think about that. And anyway, it might be the other way round. Sometimes, I almost hope that is how it will be.

If I did not know that 'Five' was sitting on top of the kitchen table, so regularly, so confidently, twice a day, waiting for his fish, I should feel that the peaceful rhythm of life had gone awry. Needless to say, the rhythm of one's life is not always so 'peaceful'; one has one's share of travails and troubles and tribulations. But in the background of my mind there is a haven to which I can retreat, and it is a haven which the three of you have created for me. It is almost as though in the stormiest of weathers, when the winds and the rains are at the height of their assaults, I had only to close my eyes and hear, in the distance, the gentle solace of a purr. Half past seven in the morning, rain or shine. Half past four in the afternoon, winter or summer. Wherever I may find myself, on land or sea, I have only to raise my wrist, and check the time, and hey presto ... there is the vision of 'Five' before me, on the kitchen table. Waiting to be served. Sitting very erect, rather as Queen Mary used to sit. Paws slightly spread out, like a ballerina at the ready. Tail hanging over the edge, giving an occasional twitch. Green eyes wide open, regarding the proceedings with interest and—what is most important—with implicit trust.

It is wonderful to see that look in your eyes, my dear 'Five'. As a man, I am not too proud of my standing, in the eyes of you and your kind. I have a guilt complex, whenever I think of the way in which men have conducted themselves towards you. We are both the creatures of God; we just happened to be born in different kingdoms. My kingdom, materially, is the more powerful, and it has exercised its power with a brutality and a cynicism which no animal would employ. You use only one pair of claws, dear 'Five', to protect yourself. You do not invent machines with a million claws, to tear out the heart of humanity. But all this, perhaps, is a little beyond the compass of our discussion.

Let me therefore thank you, once again, for the peace you have given me. Seven-thirty in the morning, four-thirty in the afternoon. The clock of life ticks on, and there you sit, daintily, precisely, waiting to be served. With that look of trust in your eyes. It is a look which gives me infinite comfort. It tells me that I have paid back just a little bit of that debt that I owe, as a man, to the wild creatures of the world.

And Oscar? Here my pen begins to falter, which perhaps is just as well. For Oscar is an unashamed sentimentalist, and I am not all that tough myself. So that when he sits on my lap, and gazes up at me with swimming eyes, and works himself up into such a frenzy of emotion that he begins, ever so faintly, to dribble, I feel sorely tempted to reciprocate. Not to the extent of actually dribbling, but at least to the extent of drooling in my mind.

How greatly impoverished would be the quiet domestic symphony without you, my very dear Oscar! How I should miss all those subtle sounds I associate with you! The sound of your paw on my bedroom window, demanding admittance. The sound of the blind running up as I prepare to let you in. The faint mew that comes from outside, as you sit on the ledge, in assumed pathos. The 'plonk' on the floor as you jump down—the feel of your cold, clean fur on the warm blankets as I clamber back to bed, and the loud rejoicing of your purr, that slowly dies down and blends into a symphony of sleep.

The conversation ... so brief but so revealing. The small talk as you plod across the lawn towards me on a summer afternoon. Mew, mew, mew ... purr ... mew ... purr ... mew. The mild protest when you come to the door of my study—usually at four o'clock—to complain that your fish has not been put out. ('But no, Oscar, it is only four o'clock, and you know that tea-time is not till half past.') The bright 'good morning' when you leap on to my bed, for the second time, with the breakfast tray. And sometimes—very rarely, thank heavens—the small cry of distress that tells me something is wrong.

And of course, the rending sound of fabric being torn as you scratch an old armchair, either in an exuberance of high spirits or as a sharp sign that you are not being given proper attention. Long ago I abandoned any attempt to cure you of this habit, just as I also abandoned the attempt to trim your claws. A brief reflection convinced me that it was cruel to do so. I love beautiful furniture, but the living must take precedence over the dead. People who put their Chippendale before their cats do not deserve to have either. As for the misguided young persons who have been hypnotized into buying modern furniture, those revolting objects, like surgical instruments, that are an offence to the eye and a menace to the behind ... such people should go on their knees and pray for an immediate onslaught of the sharpest-clawed felines to tear the horrid stuff to pieces.

But we were talking of the sounds that I associate with you, my dear Oscar. And so it is with your shifting shadows. They fall athwart the pattern of my life. Sharp and clear against the blind, as you demand entrance outside my window on a sunny morning. Dark and mysterious across the ceiling as you sit by the log fire in winter; they dance in time to the flickering flames, leaping, retreating, pouncing—as though you were chasing invisible mice. Perhaps the shadow I love most of all is thrown late of a summer evening, when the sun is sinking behind the hills, and when the dark pattern of trees, falling across the lawn, is monstrously elongated, as though in a distorting mirror. Then, as you walk towards me, you are followed by a strange, ghostly companion, with a tail ten feel long, and sometimes you pause and look round and stare at it ... and for a moment I can almost imagine that once again you are a kitten, and that you will start to chase it. Well ... you are no longer a kitten, and I am not growing any younger, so that these phantom pursuits can only be followed in the mind. But it is fun to think about, is it not, my dear Oscar? It has always been fun, and always will.

And so . . . 'thanks for the memory' . . . all three of you. As the result of our close and mystic companionship—for mystic indeed it is—we were all of us, I hope, a little happier and wiser than we should have been if our paths had not met. On my side, I can say that with my hand on my heart. I should feel very proud if you could say it too, in your separate ways, with your paws on your chests.